An Annotated

GUIDE TO TACTICS

An Annotated

GUIDE TO TACTICS

Carl von Clausewitz's *Theory of the Combat*

Edited and annotated
by Olivia A. Garard

MARINE CORPS UNIVERSITY PRESS
Quantico, Virginia
2021

LIBRARY OF CONGRESS CATALOGING-IN-PUBLICATION DATA

Names: Clausewitz, Carl von, 1780–1831. | Garard, Olivia A., 1991– editor. | Marine Corps University (U.S.) Press, issuing body.

Title: An annotated Guide to tactics : Carl von Clausewitz's Theory of the combat / edited and annotated by Olivia A. Garard.

Other titles: Leitfaden zur Bearbeitung der Taktik der Gefectslehre. English | Carl von Clausewitz's Theory of the combat

Description: First edition. | Quantico, Virginia : Marine Corps University Press, 2021.| Includes bibliographical references and index. | Summary: "The philosophy on which the Marine Corps' seminal warfighting doctrine is based rests on a tradition of professional military scholarship that reaches back to Carl von Clausewitz, author of the well-known treatise On War. Clausewitz's lesser-known and often-misunderstood Guide to Tactics, republished here for the first time as a standalone English text with critical annotations, houses the common tenets on which the Marine Corps' warfighting philosophy is based and provides a guide to thinking about the nature of tactics and combat as valuable to the modern warfighter as to those of old"—Provided by publisher.

Identifiers: LCCN 2021011565 | ISBN 9781732003132 (paperback)

Subjects: LCSH: Clausewitz, Carl von, 1780–1831. Leitfaden zur Bearbeitung der Taktik der Gefectslehre—Criticism, Textual. | Tactics. | Strategy. | Combat.

Classification: LCC U165.C5313 2021 | DDC 355.42—dc23 | SUDOC D 214.502:T 11

LC record available at https://lccn.loc.gov/2021011565

Published by
Marine Corps University Press
2044 Broadway Street
Quantico, VA 22134
First edition, 2021
Second printing, 2022
Third printing, 2023

ISBN: 978-1-7320031-3-2
DOI: 10.56686/9781732003132

CONTENTS

FOREWORD

Rediscovering timeless wisdom should always be treasured, especially in warfare, where such instances are few and far between. *Warfighting*, Marine Corps Doctrinal Publication (MCDP) 1, is the entry point for all Marines to begin learning about war, warfare, and combat—the core of the Marine Corps. The philosophy on which *Warfighting* is based rests on a tradition of military professional scholarship that reaches back to Carl von Clausewitz and further, too, to Sun Tzu. While Clausewitz wrote abstract, theoretical works, he continued a practice, stretching back to Caesar and Thucydides, of military professionals writing about the wars of their time and the lessons they drew therefrom.

Clausewitz lived through the entirety of the Napoleonic Wars (1803–15), first seeing combat at the age of 12 as a lance corporal and eventually rising to the rank of major general. In that time, Napoleon Bonaparte rose to power, conquered a continent, fell, rose to power, and fell again at Waterloo, a campaign in which Clausewitz personally participated. Yet, no matter how much we study the wars of Napoleon, we can never understand them as a participant, except through the writings of those who did partake. It is the vicarious experience of reading that builds up our repertoire when our direct, personal experience is short. Clausewitz, like the many other military professionals before him, strove to pass on the lessons of earlier times, asking only that we pick up books, read them, and think about what we might learn from them.

Mostly known for his masterpiece, *On War*, Clausewitz reminds Marines that war is a continuation of politics by other means. To act or to fail to act in combat has strategic consequences that are only magnified in this information-dominated age. But the hard, dirty work of combat, of Marines, persists. Strategy is only possible through the tactics that carry it out. Warfare, at its core, is about closing with and destroying the enemy by fire and maneuver. This is what *Warfighting* tells us. This is also what Clausewitz's *Guide to Tactics* explains.

The following republication of Clausewitz's *Guide to Tactics* should seem familiar to Marines because it houses the common tenets on which our warfighting philosophy is based. But it is also a bit different too. It is more abstract; it wrestles with questions such as what is combat, what is the offense, and what is a plan. As we face the unceasing, continued evolution of the character of warfare it is worth reflecting on these basics—the underlying theory of tactics—to understand how they are manifesting in the current competition and how they will manifest in the next fight.

The military profession is one of lifelong learning. It is a continual process of interrogation and challenging oneself: *Where do I need improvement?* This is a mental as well as a physical pursuit. Reexamining the foundations of warfare and combat, on which much of our philosophy rests, is a necessary and valuable process. This new-old work helps to reground principles that we, as Marines, know and love, like fires and maneuver; clarify differences between the offense and the defense; and show the beginning of what became mission command.

We must take it upon ourselves to wrestle this text to the ground and squeeze out all the nuance we can. The best texts will resist submission and always allow us to wring out more. That is why we reread *Warfighting*. The salient points that stand out at the beginning of your career will not be the same ones that stick out at the end of your career, whenever that may be. This is also true of *Guide to Tactics*. Tackle this text hard and see what you can wrest from it. Then read it again; it wants another bout.

Major General Julian Dale Alford
Commanding General,
Marine Corps Installations East/Marine Corps Base Camp Lejeune

PREFACE

Carl von Clausewitz's ideas are well known, if perhaps not well studied, in the military profession. His view of war as an expression of scholarship is essentially canon among military professionals, regardless of nation. Even al-Qaeda studies Clausewitz.[1] For all his influence on modern ideas of war and strategy, however, his tactical concepts have been strangely ignored.

We know how Clausewitz viewed the relationship between tactics and strategy from *On War*. It is well attested at various points: tactics, or combat, are the means of strategy. Tactics achieve (or fail to achieve) victories on the battlefield and strategy is the use of those victories to impose a political end state on the defeated party. We also know his conception of war as a phenomenon: political discourse with the addition of violence. *On War*, his masterpiece, thus captures both war and strategy as phenomena, but does not capture tactics as a phenomenon. There is some belief that he intended to write such a work, but he was never able to do so.[2]

Because of his focus on war and strategy in *On War*, his thoughts on tactics as a phenomenon are best captured in this earlier work, *Guide to Tactics*. We cannot be certain exactly when he wrote it or why, or whether he would have expanded it later in life, but we do know what it is and what it is not.

First, what it is not: *Guide to Tactics* is not doctrine. Doctrine is the codified tactics, techniques, and procedures of a specific military force for specific situations, equipment, and unit organizations.[3] This work was not produced as a piece of Prussian Army doctrine. Nor is it a simple tactical polemic, containing the author's opinion on what tactics are good or bad or necessary.

---

[1] Brett A. Friedman, "Mujahideen: The Strategic Tradition of Sunni Jihadism," *Small Wars Journal*, 28 October 2015.

[2] Raymond Aron, *Penser la guerre, Clausewitz*, tome 2, *L'âge planétaire* (Paris: Gallimard, 1976), 339.

[3] B. A. Friedman, *On Tactics: A Theory of Victory in Battle* (Annapolis, MD: Naval Institute Press, 2017).

It is a guide to thinking about the nature of tactics; the difference is subtle but important. That is what makes it theory and not doctrine or a manual. Its purpose is to train the mind of the reader to think critically about what tactics are so that they can be better prepared to choose effective tactics in practice. Some of these tactical concepts reappear in *On War*, while others do not. But modern readers will perhaps recognize all of them.

The Purpose of Tactics: Victory

Clausewitz defined tactics and strategy in terms of logic: the logic of tactics is winning on the battlefield, and the logic of strategy is to use those victories as means to achieve the ends of the war. In other words, the means must always be used in service of the ends. This practice pertains to today in the form of the familiar ends, ways, and means depiction of strategy.[4] The resources necessary to perform a mission and the ways in which they will be applied toward its completion are unified by the end goal or object. The insertion of *ways* is a later addition, but for both tactics and strategy the means and the ends play heavily in Clausewitz's thinking.

In *Guide to Tactics*, the end or object of tactics is victory, defined as the withdrawal of the enemy force from the battle (see page 30). The means is combat, which, in Clausewitz's vision, entails both organized violence and the threat thereof (see page 36). In *On War*, the means in general remain combat, although the word *combat* is sometimes used interchangeably with *battle* and *engagement*.[5] *Tactics* is defined as "the theory of the use of military forces in combat."[6] This still implies that the purpose is victory, which is spelled out in *Guide to Tactics* but left implied in *On War*.

What differentiates tactics from strategy is the ends of both activities. The means for strategy are the same, but the ends are

[4] This is the Lykke Model of Strategy (strategy = ends + ways + means), named for Arthur F. Lykke Jr. Also see *The Marine Corps War College Strategy Primer* (Quantico, VA: Marine Corps University Press, 2021).
[5] See Gen Carl von Clausewitz, *On War*, trans. Col J. J. Graham, vol. 1, book 1, chap. 2 (London: Kega Paul, Trench, Trubner, 1918).
[6] Clausewitz, *On War*, vol. 1, book 2, chap. 1, 86.

different. The results of combat, the outcome of engagements, must contribute to the purpose of the war: the political aim. Clausewitz defines strategy as "the theory of the use of combats for the object of the War."[7] In other words, while the means of tactics and strategy are the same, the aim of tactics is strictly to win on the battlefield, but the aim of strategy is to contribute to the political goal of the eventual peace.

Clausewitz thus sets up a dilemma: tactics and strategy have different and sometimes diametrically opposed ends. The means, however, are the same: combat. And combat is inherently destructive and violent. Achieving the aim of tactics is pretty straightforward given the means: the destruction, in whole or in part, of the opposing force yields victory in combat. In strategy, however, the aim is peace. It may be a peace imposed on the opponent, one that is advantageous to the victor, but it is peace nonetheless. The dilemma is how inherently destructive and violent means can lead, through tactics and strategy, to inherently peaceful ends. The solution to this paradoxical dilemma is deceptively simple in theory but difficult in practice. To make the violent means in war contribute to peaceful ends, those peaceful ends must be kept in mind and take priority in military decisions. In his words,

> Strategy is the employment of the battle to gain the end of the War; it must therefore give an aim to the whole military action, which must be in accordance with the object of the War; in other words, Strategy forms the plan of the War, and to this end it links together the series of acts which are to lead to the final decision, that is to say it makes the plans for the separate campaigns and *regulates* the combat to be fought in each.[8]

This regulatory function of strategy over tactics is necessary to achieve the aim of the war.

---

[7] Clausewitz, *On War*, vol. 1, book 2, chap. 1, 86.
[8] Clausewitz, *On War*, vol. 1, book 3, chap. 1, 165, emphasis added.

The practical application of this theoretical concept is that a commander must always keep strategy in mind and make it the priority over tactical concerns. While it may make sense tactically, for example, to be totally ruthless with the enemy forces and pursue them vigorously until they are totally destroyed, even to the point of executing prisoners and wounded, it is strategically counterproductive (not to mention morally reprehensible). While tactics is only concerned with combat, strategy must also be concerned with the eventual peace. An opponent who has seen their soldiers and civilians massacred will be less inclined to negotiate and make peace and will instead refuse to submit to the will of the opponent. Resolving this paradox is the goal of strategists and policy makers, but their efforts cannot be undermined by tacticians and practitioners.

Close Combat and Fire Combat

The subordinate relationship of tactics to strategy is necessary context, but it is not directly addressed in *Guide to Tactics* as it is strictly focused on tactics. The centerpiece of Clausewitz's thought on combat itself are two modes of combat: fire combat and close combat.

Close combat is a phrase with which every Marine is familiar through the mission of the Marine Corps rifle squad, which is: "To locate, close with, and destroy the enemy by fire and maneuver, or repel the enemy's assault by fire and close combat."[9] That mission statement and Clausewitz's term are, perhaps surprisingly, referring to exactly the same thing: the direct clash of opposing infantry units resolved through combat at bayonet range.

For Clausewitz, close combat is defined by its certainty. The only way to be certain that an enemy force is defeated is to force it off its position and seize that position instead. It also creates an impression of certainty in the mind of the enemy combatants, generating more fear and a sense of danger than fire combat. Nothing accomplishes this feat like an infantry assault.

---

[9] *Marine Rifle Squad*, Marine Corps Interim Publication 3-10A.4i w/change 1 (Washington, DC: Headquarters Marine Corps, 2019), 7.

Fire combat, however, is the use of supporting arms and, today, crew-served weapons. Clausewitz viewed fire combat as including the preparatory shelling of enemy positions by artillery and the massed fire of infantry units in formation (prior to a bayonet charge) as fire combat.

There are obviously a lot more options for supporting arms today than there were during Clausewitz's time, but the nature of fire combat remains the same: it is probabilistic. Even precision-guided weapons only have a high probability of hitting the target, never a certainty. That lack of certainty means that fire combat can never be as decisive as close combat (which achieves certainty by physically replacing the enemy on a given piece of terrain). The enemy force being subjected to fire combat knows that there is a chance they will escape, hide, or otherwise avoid the effects of fire combat because there is only a probability, not a certainty, of their own death or wounding. The fear experienced by the enemy force subjected to fire combat is different, on a visceral level, from that experienced in close combat. It is not pleasant, as those experienced in it will attest, but it is different.

The practical value of these concepts lies in the realm of planning. Some Marines may be familiar with the planning construct of a shaping phase, a decisive phase, and a sustaining phase.[10] While there is no sustaining phase in *Guide to Tactics*, fire combat is clearly the shaping phase and close combat is clearly the decisive phase of combat.

The coordination and combination of both fire combat and close combat is, of course, combined arms. Clausewitz viewed fire combat and close combat as two distinct phases. This reflects the tactics of the time before reliable, aimed rifle fire and indirect artillery. The need to fire artillery pieces directly and by sight and then move them out of the way or cease firing while the infantry forces conducted sometimes intricate and complex maneuvers in formation required a segmented plan to every battle. However, the interaction between the two—the modern concept of

---

[10] See *Tactics*, Marine Corps Doctrinal Publication (MCDP) 1-3 (Washington, DC: Headquarters Marine Corps, 1997), especially chap. 2 and 7.

combined arms—is inherent in his theory even though he could have hardly conceived of modern combined arms warfare featuring indirect artillery fire, fixed-wing and rotary-wing aircraft, other armored vehicles, and, now, autonomous systems.

The point of combined arms in Clausewitz's view and in modern military doctrine is that both fire combat (supporting arms) and close combat (maneuver) are more powerful in combination—one supporting and facilitating the other in turn—than they are when used by themselves. Fire combat cannot bring about a decision on the battlefield. Close combat can but only in limited circumstances (usually when one side vastly outnumbers the other). Both in concert, however, can deliver a decision.

Attack and Defense

The concepts of fire combat and close combat pertain to both attack and defense, both of which will involve fire combat and close combat. The core of Clausewitz's thoughts on attack and defense, later captured in *On War*, are already present in *Guide to Tactics*.

Famously, Clausewitz stated that the defense is the stronger form of fighting. By stronger, he is not necessarily saying it is better, merely that because the defense can stay in place, rested and ready, and take advantage of force multipliers like fortifications and terrain, the offense needs a preponderance of combat power to overcome a defense. If both sides are equal, the defense will win.

However, the defense can never gain anything. It can only keep possession of ground already controlled. Only the offense can gain anything. In *Guide to Tactics*, he states that the offense is the positive mode and defense is the negative mode for these reasons. He does not mean good or bad, just that the offense is necessary to gain ground against the enemy, and the defense is necessary to hold it. He goes on to say that the offense will contain a greater proportion of close combat than fire combat, and the defense will be reversed, containing more fire combat and less close combat.

Command and Control

The concept of *Auftragstaktik*, known today as mission command, is not normally associated with Clausewitz. It does not appear in *On War*, but the germ of the German tradition of decentralized command and control is evident in *Guide to Tactics*.

Clausewitz first discusses planning for combat engagements. While he certainly believes in planning engagements beforehand, he does not believe that any plan can be perfect, given the unpredictable nature of combat and the human element. He states:

> But belligerents do not cease to be men, and individuals can never be converted into machines having no will of their own; and the ground on which they fight will seldom or never be a complete and bare level, which can exercise no influence on the combat. It is, therefore, quite impossible to calculate beforehand all that is to take place. . . . As for the plan for a great battle, except as regards the preliminary part, it can only ever be a very general outline.[11] (See p. 64)

This is an argument for the use of mission-type orders; assigning subordinate units a mission to accomplish without mandating how it must be accomplished.[12] Mission-type orders are a vital component of mission command. The other main component—commander's intent—is a later concept that does not appear in Clausewitz's work.

Connections to *Warfighting*, Marine Corps Doctrinal Publication (MCDP) 1

Familiarity with Clausewitz's views on war can help Marines better understand and implement *Warfighting* for the simple reason that *Warfighting* is fundamentally Clausewitzian. Various theorists influenced its contents, including Sir Basil Liddell Hart and especially Air Force pilot John R. Boyd. But it is rooted at a

---

[11] Clausewitz, *On War*, vol. 3, appendix, propositions 103–4, 260.
[12] Compare B. A. Friedman and Olivia A. Garard, "Clarifying Command: Keeping up with the (John Paul) Joneses," *War on the Rocks*, 7 April 2020.

foundational level in Clausewitz; he is the first theorist cited by name in the document.

The purpose of *On War* was to define war as a phenomenon and the essential aspects of that definition are adopted in *Warfighting*. These include that war is an expression of politics with the addition of violent means; that war is a human phenomenon and the human element cannot be ignored in theory or in practice; that warfare is inherently competitive, complex, uncertain, and chaotic; and that war's physical aspects exist alongside mental and moral aspects, all of which are powerful in different ways. In fact, *Warfighting* is divided into four chapters: "The Nature of War," "The Theory of War," "Preparing for War," and "The Conduct of War." These aspects of war all have their origin in Clausewitz's ideas and the phrases themselves appear in his works.

These connections between *On War* and *Warfighting* are well known, but the resurfacing of *Guide to Tactics* has highlighted even more connections between Clausewitzian thinking and the Marine Corps' warfighting philosophy. Two concepts that do not appear in *On War* but do appear, in nascent form, in *Guide to Tactics* are decentralized decision making and combined arms.

Clausewitz's heavy focus on the two forms of combat—fire and close combat—could have easily led to an attritionist mindset overly concerned with casualties, body counts, and loss of materiel. Clausewitz, however, never went down that road because of the conception of decision, formulated first at the beginning of this work when he defines victory as a decision in the mind of one of the belligerents, either the commander or the commanded. He does not shy away from saying that the destruction of the enemy force may indeed be the aim of combat. Sometimes it is. But he also does not say it is the only way. Indeed, he goes to great lengths to repeat that it is not always the case.

Clausewitz has been criticized as being focused on attrition and overly focused on direct approaches for nearly a century. This is a result of critics working with only a part of his work. Between Clausewitz's heavy focus on mental and moral forces in war, evident in *On War*, and now the roots of modern concepts found in *Guide to Tactics*, Clausewitz can be revealed as much more of a maneuverist than an attritionist.

Conclusion

In the twentieth century, strategy became of vital importance not just because of the two world wars but thereafter, as confrontation with the Soviet Union defined the rest of the century. In 1976, when Michael Howard and Peter Paret's translation of Clausewitz's *On War* was published, it hit at a time when American academics and military practitioners were vitally concerned with strategy after the defeat in Vietnam.

Since then, strategy in general and Clausewitz's views on strategy in particular have received all the attention, at the expense of the theory of tactics. Tactical theory was relegated to doctrine instead of theory, usually appearing in the form of a list of the principles of war, of which there are many different versions. But theory fits poorly into doctrine for a simple reason: theory should inform doctrine, not the other way around. The poor state of tactical theory is a problem. Strategy can only be accomplished through tactics, and it will never be properly understood without an understanding of tactics.

That *Guide to Tactics*, and *Warfighting* for that matter, are works of theory and not doctrine explains their timeless nature. They are not tied to the ever-changing character of war in a certain time and place but rather to the unchanging nature of war. They do not seek to tell us what to do, but rather to teach us how to think about their subject. Military service is a thinking profession, so this restoration of *Guide to Tactics* as a stand-alone work of military theory is of value across the profession.

B. A. Friedman

An Annotated

GUIDE TO TACTICS

UNLOCKING *GUIDE TO TACTICS*

ne of the unfortunate side effects of the deserved success of Carl von Clausewitz's *On War* is that it has overshadowed the other works of this preeminent philosopher of war. But perhaps none of Clausewitz's writings are as undercited and underread as his *Guide to Tactics*, republished here with critical annotations for the first time as a stand-alone English text.[1] Likely written between 1808 and 1812, while Clausewitz was working for Gerhard Johann David von Scharnhorst at the Berlin War Academy (*Kriegsschule*), *Guide to Tactics* stands in stark contrast to his better-known but lesser text of that same time, *Principles of War*.[2] Unlike *Principles of War*, which was a summary of Clausewitz's instructions to the Prussian crown prince (a teenage Friedrich Wilhelm IV), *Guide to Tactics* reads with an eye toward posterity, like *On War*. Both are deeply theoretical works, the former a theory of combat, the latter a theory of war. In a note written around 1818, Clausewitz hoped his "small volume in octavo," which eventually became *On War*, "would not be forgotten after two or three years."[3] *On War*, published posthumously in 1832 by Marie von Clausewitz, his wife, has lived up to that aspiration. That *Guide to Tactics* has not is mostly due to accidents of literary history.

On War is Clausewitz's most famous work, from which are derived key aphorisms like War is a Continuation of Politics

---

[1] *Guide to Tactics, or the Theory of the Combat* in German is *Leitfaden zur Bearbeitung der Taktik der Gefechtslehre*. Carl von Clausewitz, *Vom Kriege, Hinterlassenes Werk des Generals Carl von Clausewitz*, ed. Werner Hahlweg, 18th ed. (Bonn, Germany: Dümmler, 1973), 1103–80; and Carl von Clausewitz, *On War*, trans. Col J. J. Graham (New York: Barnes and Noble, 2004), appendix, 798–870. The text in this book is taken from Gen Carl von Clausewitz, *On War*, trans. Col J. J. Graham (London: Kegan Paul, Trench, Trubner, 1918), 243–337. This introduction builds on thoughts originally expressed in Olivia Garard, "Clausewitzian Deep Tracks: #Reviewing Guide to Tactics, or the Theory of the Combat," *Strategy Bridge*, 23 March 2020.

[2] Hew Strachan, *Clausewitz's* On War: *A Biography* (New York: Grove Press, 2007), 118. The *Kriegsschule* is the forerunner to the *Kriegsakademie* at which Clausewitz taught in his later years. Strachan, *Clausewitz's* On War, 49.

[3] Carl von Clausewitz, *On War*, ed. and trans. Michael Howard and Peter Paret (Princeton, NJ: Princeton University Press, 1984), 63.

with Other Means.[4] This has been the text that has defined what war is for generations of military members and has illustrated strategy's relationship to policy. Since Clausewitz died prior to a complete revision of the eight books of *On War*, scholars debate, among other nuanced issues, the extent to which his thought is logically consistent or continuous, which parts of the work represent his revised thought, the extent of his intellectual crisis of 1827, and the primary lessons to take away.[5] *On War* is lengthy, long-winded, and philosophically sophisticated.[6] For Clausewitz, it was through the interplay of historical analysis and lived experience that war's essence emerged.[7] *Guide to Tactics* is formally different. It is intellectually complex and abstract, without *On War*'s historical grounding; though there are many threads linking *Guide to Tactics* to *On War*, the two texts are not interchangeable but, rather, complementary. *Guide to Tactics* serves both as a theoretical work on combat and the core substance from which we can develop a deeper understanding of *On War*.

On War is not the apotheosis of *Guide to Tactics*. That appellation would suggest that all the critical concepts of *On War* find a kernel in *Guide to Tactics*, which is too strong a claim and

---

[4] In Werner Hahlweg's edition, Clausewitz writes, "der Krieg ist nichts als eine Fortsetzung des politischen Verkehrs mit Einmischung anderer Mittel." Clausewitz, *Vom Kriege*, 990. In Col J. J. Graham's translation, this reads as "War is nothing but a continuation of political intercourse, with a mixture of other means." Clausewitz, *On War*, trans. Graham, vol. 3, book 8, chap. 6, 121.

[5] W. B. Gallie, "Clausewitz Today," *European Journal of Sociology* 19, no. 1 (1978): 146, https://doi.org/10.1017/S0003975600005130. In one of the most damning of philosophical critiques, Gallie then levies: "Clausewitz begs the question." Gallie, "Clausewitz Today," 153. Compare Strachan, who makes explicit the intellectual departure occurring in Clausewitz's works between 1812 and 1827. Strachan, *Clausewitz's* On War, 74–75. Conversely, Paret sees continuity from 1804 to 1830. Peter Paret, *Clausewitz and the State: The Man, His Theories, and His Times* (Princeton, NJ: Princeton University Press, 2007), 8. See also Youri Cormier, *War as Paradox: Clausewitz and Hegel on Fighting Doctrines and Ethics* (Montreal: McGill-Queen's University Press, 2016), 11; Eugenio Diniz and Domício Proença Júnior, "A Criterion for Settling Inconsistencies in Clausewitz's *On War*," *Journal of Strategic Studies* 37, no. 6–7 (2014): 897, https://doi-org.lomc.idm.oclc.org/10.1080/01402390.2011.621725; Beatrice Heuser, *Reading Clausewitz* (London: Random House, 2002), 32; Strachan, *Clausewitz's* On War, 26; and Christopher Coker, *Rebooting Clausewitz:* On War *in the 21st Century* (New York: Oxford University Press, 2017), 148.

[6] Jon Tetsuro Sumida, *Decoding Clausewitz: A New Approach to* On War (Lawrence: University Press of Kansas, 2008), 67.

[7] C. B. A. Behrens, "Which Side Was Clausewitz On?," *New York Review of Books*, 14 October 1976.

ignores the natural evolution of Clausewitz's thought as well as the poetics of *On War*.[8] Raymond Aron considers *Guide to Tactics* methodologically, conceptually, and empirically consistent with *On War*.[9] Jan Willem Honig makes the point, however, that "if one views *On War* as the consistent, coherent, and essentially complete summation of Clausewitz's thought, and regards his other works as preparing the way for his *magnum opus*, then there may not be much point in publishing more, other than to provide some additional illustrations for issues already familiar."[10] Instead, *Guide to Tactics* should be seen as a completion of the foundation on which rests many of the premises refined in *On War*. This difference is key. *Guide to Tactics* infuses *On War* with more meaning; it is an expansion from within the text itself.[11] Concepts found within *Guide to Tactics* find their full maturation or transcendence in *On War*. *On War* is both consistent with and a step beyond and beside *Guide to Tactics*. Essentially, *Guide to Tactics* is the missing link to many completed concepts within *On War*—most notably, that of the combat.

What Is the Theory of the Combat?

In the foreword to the French translation of *Leitfaden zur Bearbeitung der Taktik der Gefectslehre* (*Guide to Tactics, or the Theory of the Combat*), Hervé Coutau-Bégarie, the president of L'Institut

---

[8] See Anders Engberg-Pedersen, *Empire of Chance: The Napoleonic Wars and the Disorder of Things* (Cambridge, MA: Harvard University Press, 2015). Sumida goes further because "he examines *On War* as a theory of practice rather than as a theory of a phenomenon." Sumida, *Decoding Clausewitz*, 2.

[9] Raymond Aron, *Penser la guerre, Clausewitz*, tome 1, *L'âge européen* (Paris: Gallimard, 1976), 30.

[10] Jan Willem Honig, "Interpreting Clausewitz," *Security Studies* 3, no. 3 (Spring 1994): 573, https://doi.org/10.1080/09636419409347562.

[11] Further research is necessary to track the evolution of specific concepts. For instance, in the last proposition, Clausewitz sees a commander's character—specifically, their resolution—as the only way to govern chance and prevent "half measures." Clausewitz, *On War*, trans. Graham, vol. 3, appendix, prop. 604, 337. Here, Clausewitz is concerned with an individual commander's trepidation in warfare. In *On War*, Clausewitz is concerned with (and intrigued by) "half-and-half" or "half-hearted" affairs of the *state*. See Honig's full discussion on the various translations of this concept. Jan Willem Honig, "Clausewitz's *On War*: Problems of Text and Translation," *Clausewitz in the Twenty-First Century*, ed. Hew Strachan and Andreas Herberg-Rothe (Oxford: Oxford University Press, 2007), 68nn35–36, https://doi.org/10.1093/acprof:oso/9780199232024.003.0004.

de Stratégie Comparée, the French think tank that republished the text, begins from a fundamental question: How should one translate *Gefecht*?[12] Its translation has been disputed.[13] For instance, Paul Schuurman translates the title as "Outline to work on the tactics of the doctrine of combat."[14] Conversely, although Hew Strachan only refers to *Guide to Tactics* by its German title, he has an extensive discussion on the differences between *Kampf* (combat), *Gefecht* (engagement), and *Schlacht* (battle).[15] Strachan observes that Clausewitz avoided *Kampf*, but he used *Gefecht* to differentiate between "the fighting which is not in itself decisive" and a *Schlacht*, a battle that is.[16] Moreover, he specifically references how *Gefecht* is the title of book 4, which is, as he translates, the book on "the engagement." However, other translations render this as the book on "the combat."[17]

Regardless of whether it should be translated as a theory of combat or a theory of engagement, the *Guide to Tactics* is a work on tactics. In *On Tactics*, B. A. Friedman writes that "a theory of tactics must be timeless and applicable to any battle, anywhere, anytime."[18] "Tactics," Friedman further defines, "is the arrangement of military forces in such a manner to defeat the enemy."[19] This is consistent with, and derivative from, Clausewitz's defini-

---

[12] Hervé Coutau-Bégarie, "Avant-Propos," in Carl von Clausewitz, *Théorie du Combat*, trans. Thomas Lindemann (Paris: Economica, 1998), 7. Lindemann comes down on Graham's, Hans Gatzke's, and Paul Schuurman's sides: combat.

[13] Book 4 of *Vom Kriege* is *Das Gefecht*. Clausewitz, *Vom Kriege*, 417. Graham translates this as "the combat." Clausewitz, *On War*, trans. Graham, vol. 1, book 4, 235. Howard and Paret and Jolles translate it as "the engagement." Clausewitz, *On War*, trans. Howard and Paret, 223, and trans. Jolles, 451. In *Principles of War*, however, Gatzke translates chapter 2, *Taktik oder Gefectslehre*, as "Tactics or the Theory of the Combat." Carl von Clausewitz, *Principles of War*, trans. Hans W. Gatzke (Harrisburg, PA: Military Service Publishing, 1942), 15.

[14] Paul Schuurman, "War as a System: A Three-Stage Model for the Development of Clausewitz's Thinking on Military Conflict and Its Constraints," *Journal of Strategic Studies* 37, no. 6–7 (2014): 928n4, https://doi-org.lomc.idm.oclc.org/10.1080/01402390.2014.933316. Considering this doctrine, as argued in B. A. Friedman's preface, is problematic.

[15] *Leitfaden zur Bearbeitung der Taktik der Gefectslehre*; and Strachan, *Clausewitz's* On War, 140–41.

[16] Strachan, *Clausewitz's* On War, 140–41.

[17] Compare to note 13.

[18] B. A. Friedman, *On Tactics: A Theory of Victory in Battle* (Annapolis, MD: Naval Institute Press, 2007), x.

[19] Friedman, *On Tactics*, 16.

tion in *On War*, that "tactics *is the theory of the use of military forces in combat*."[20] Whereas in other works (such as *Principles of War*, written around the same time as *Guide to Tactics* and discussed further below), Clausewitz is focused on specifics of fighting, in *Guide to Tactics*, Clausewitz explores these more abstract conceptions of his subject matter. *Guide to Tactics* qualifies as theory because it is—except for a few noted Napoleonic tactical holdovers—evergreen.

Clausewitz is not focused on lethality itself, but rather on the *why* of lethality.[21] The why has not changed, even as the means have—the fight persists as the fighting changes. For example, a distinction Clausewitz makes in *Guide to Tactics* is between close combat and fire combat, loosely correlated to maneuver and firepower. Fire combat entails "weapons with which the enemy can be attacked while he is at a distance."[22] These are, Clausewitz continues, "more instruments for the understanding; they allow the feelings, the 'instinct for fighting' properly called, to remain almost at rest, and this so much the more according as the range of their effects is greater."[23] In other words, a weapon with great effective range, like artillery or aviation, allows a military force to affect another without subjecting their personnel to the fear and strain of close combat. Close combat, on the other hand, is that which is "nearest to the pugilistic encounter."[24] Since it is akin to maneuver, close combat is fueled by passions, whereas fire combat, or fires, is distanced—intellectually, emotionally,

---

[20] Clausewitz, *On War*, trans. Graham, vol. 1, book 2, chap. 1, 86. There is a sense in which leveraging Clausewitz's definition of tactics to judge the validity of the tactical theories in *Principles of War* or *Guide to Tactics* could be considered begging the question, but given that *On War* has been theoretically established as the paradigm from which we understand war and strategy, it seems valid that we use it to judge tactics too. Moreover, we are not leveraging this definition in order to see continuity between *On War* and either *Principles of War* or *Guide to Tactics*, but to judge each on their own merits with respect to their current applicability.

[21] See Olivia Garard, "Lethality: An Inquiry," *Strategy Bridge*, 1 November 2018. *Lethality* is defined as "an emergent, intentional relationship between an object and the surface on which it is used." Furthermore, lethality is a "latent inexorable deadly relationship between a weapon and its effects."

[22] Clausewitz, *On War*, trans. Graham, appendix, prop. 47, 250.

[23] Clausewitz, *On War*, trans. Graham, appendix, prop. 47, 250.

[24] Clausewitz, *On War*, trans. Graham, appendix, prop. 46, 250.

and literally. "Both," importantly, "have for their object the destruction of the enemy."[25] This Clausewitzian taxonomy is applicable to differentiating and understanding the ever-changing means of warfare, even as its goal remains the same.

However, the "epistemology of lethality" varies.[26] For close combat, this "effect [of destruction] is quite certain."[27] What makes it lethal is its certainty: an assured expectation of a future deadly harm.[28] Fire combat, conversely, "is only more or less probable."[29] This remains true today, even as we seek to increase our tactical precision.[30] This credence differential is critical to identifying the variance between the *destructive* act and the *decisive* act. The reason the enemy is driven from the battlefield, which is victory as a decisive act, is because of the certainty of destruction by close combat. Crucially, it is not the destruction itself. Fire combat, conversely, is only "the preparation" for a decisive act—even if, or because, it destroys the adversary's force.[31] These propositions found within *Guide to Tactics* can help to clarify the critical point Strachan highlights in the meaning of *Gefecht*: that it is not decisive in itself, but that it relies on the perception of probable destruction. *Combat*, as fighting, encompasses this sense more readily than *engagement*.

Combat, as fighting, is also at the core of *On War*.[32] There is general scholarly agreement on this point. Emile Simpson sees combat as the "vernacular of battle," which through "the language of war" unites "force to political meaning."[33] Sibylle Scheipers notes Clausewitz's "unitary conception of war," which

---

[25] Clausewitz, *On War*, trans. Graham, appendix, prop. 50, 250.

[26] Matthew Ford, "The Epistemology of Lethality: Bullets, Knowledge Trajectories, Kinetic Effects," *European Journal of International Security* 5, no. 1 (February 2020): 77, https://doi.org/10.1017/eis.2019.12.

[27] Clausewitz, *On War*, trans. Graham, appendix, prop. 51, 250.

[28] See Garard, "Lethality."

[29] Clausewitz, *On War*, trans. Graham, appendix, prop. 51, 250.

[30] Compare Olivia Garard, "Targeting Clausewitzian Judgments: Fusing Precision and Accuracy to Strategy and Tactics," *Strategy Bridge*, 20 September 2016. Consider how the military uses the concepts of probability of incapacitation or the probability of hit.

[31] Clausewitz, *On War*, trans. Graham, appendix, prop. 60, 252.

[32] Clausewitz, *On War*, trans. Graham, vol. 1, book 4, chap. 3, 238–43.

[33] Emile Simpson, *War from the Ground Up: Twenty-First-Century Combat as Politics* (London: Hurst, 2012), 15.

holds that "all wars are defined by one basic, unifying feature: combat or at least the possibility of combat."[34] Antulio J. Echevarria II, too, explicitly sees "*On War* [as] a combat-centric theory of war."[35]

Clausewitz defines tactics as the conduct of individual combats, while strategy is their use.[36] And yet, despite the primacy of combat in *On War*, Strachan remarks that "Clausewitz barely mentioned tactics in *On War*."[37] This omission is complicated by the fact that "strategic success [is] conditional on tactical success, [such] that tactics lead and even dominate strategy."[38] Extending this dyad to include policy, Anders Engberg-Pedersen and Martin Kornberger frame the relationship between tactics and policy as "how that which is possible shapes action and how action delimits what is imagined as possible."[39] The *possibilities* are delineated by tactics, while that which is *desired* is determined by policy.[40] Without *Guide to Tactics*, a reading of *On War* has not been conditioned on what is possible. This error represents a fundamental misunderstanding between tactics and strategy. In many ways, those who enact strategy believe that they are abstracted away from the tactics, beyond the dirty work of warfare. But that is not true. Strategy resides in the interface between political desires and tactical attempts, uniting the two but bounded by their scope.[41] In fact, the relationship between the texts *Guide to Tactics* and *On War* mimics the relationship between tactics and strategy. *Guide to Tactics* is a theory of the

---

[34] Sibylle Scheipers, *On Small War: Carl von Clausewitz and People's War* (Oxford, UK: Oxford University Press, 2018), 1, https://doi.org/10.1093/oso/9780198799047.001.0001.

[35] Antulio J. Echevarria II, "Combat, War's only Means," in *Clausewitz and Contemporary War* (New York: Oxford University Press, 2007), 141, https://doi.org/10.1093/acprof:oso/9780199231911.001.0001.

[36] Clausewitz, *On War*, trans. Graham, vol. 1, book 2, chap. 1, 86.

[37] Strachan, *Clausewitz's* On War, 117.

[38] Strachan, *Clausewitz's* On War, 117.

[39] Anders Engberg-Pedersen and Martin Kornberger, "Reading Clausewitz, Reimagining the Practice of Strategy," *Strategic Organization* 1, no. 13 (June 2019): 8, https://doi.org/10.1177/1476127019854963. See also Simpson, *War from the Ground Up*, 116.

[40] Engberg-Pedersen and Kornberger, "Reading Clausewitz, Reimagining the Practice of Strategy," 8.

[41] Engberg-Pedersen and Kornberger, "Reading Clausewitz, Reimagining the Practice of Strategy," 7. See also Olivia Garard, "The Interface: Reestablishing the Relationship Between Tactics and Politics," *War Room*, 20 August 2020.

combat; *On War* is a theory of its use. Both must be instigated and guided by policy.

The insights Clausewitz gleaned from his study of combat in *Guide to Tactics* he settled within the very fabric of *On War* and then extended as he widened his lens from combat to war, in which combat transpires.[42] The "philosophical-dialectical method" with which Clausewitz constructed *On War*, and which is particularly acute in the relationship between war and policy, is at work, too, in his exploration of the nature of combat.[43] For one, the relationship between tactics and strategy, as Strachan rightly notes, is the dialectic found in "the central books of *On War*."[44] Next, Clausewitz investigates the interaction between what is possible (tactics) and what is desired (policy), which "resolves itself in new and more complex questions and paradoxes."[45] These dialectical interactions both compose strategy and pose for strategy the question of what it seeks to sort out. How to balance the art of the possible at the behest of the desired is what *On War* sought to unravel, with *Guide to Tactics*, as an attempt to theoretically articulate that *possible*, embedded at its core.

What therefore differentiates *Guide to Tactics* most among Clausewitz's works is how it situates itself in relation to *On War*. In many ways, it serves as its inverse. Given that *On War* functions to describe the relationship of war to politics, *Guide to Tactics* describes the relationship of tactics to war. Strategy—the interface between policy and tactics—infuses *Guide to Tactics* with its purpose and initiative, limited, as we know from *On War*, by the extent of policy. To understand war requires analysis on both sides of the interface. That means a balanced understanding between *On War* and *Guide to Tactics* is necessary. *On War* expanded *Guide to Tactics*'s immediacy of combat to war as a whole. Yet, a reading of *On War* without the grounding in the logic and limits of combat offered by *Guide to Tactics* is incom-

---

[42] Scheipers, *On Small War*, 37.
[43] Scheipers, *On Small War*, 37.
[44] Strachan, *Clausewitz's* On War, 107.
[45] Cormier, *War as Paradox*, 19–20.

plete.[46] Without both, our understanding of war and warfare is impoverished.

Still, the text of *Guide to Tactics* is pragmatic and relevant in and of itself, even as—or especially because—it remains theoretical. As Christopher Coker explains, "We still read [Clausewitz]—as we do all great writers—only because we find in him something his contemporaries did not."[47] There remains in Clausewitz a treasure trove of insights. And although, like *On War*, *Guide to Tactics* focuses on some specific tactics of the Napoleonic era, it treats the concepts abstractly. These formulations provide the theoretical distance necessary to apply Clausewitz's ideas beyond the specificity of the time in which he wrote it. Much like Sun Tzu's *The Art of War*, it is a work rooted in its context that nevertheless contains timeless insights. Christopher Bassford contends that

> Clausewitz has provided the intellectual common ground that formal doctrine has always sought but—because of its unavoidably narrow focus, single-service orientation, and prescriptive intent—failed to provide. The value of that common ground lies in the very flexibility of Clausewitzian theory that many have found so frustrating: It provides a common set of concepts and intellectual tools that greatly facilitate analysis and discussion while leaving the con-

---

[46] Compare to the chapter entitled "Combat, War's only Means," in which Echevarria never cites *Guide to Tactics* when exploring how important combat or the threat of it is as the means of war. Echevarria, *Clausewitz and Contemporary War*, 133–53. Given *Guide to Tactics*'s relationship to *On War*, he is not incorrect in his assessment, but further details are missed. For instance, Clausewitz's summary of victory in *On War*, which considers three factors, is a further abstraction of his seven factors in *Guide to Tactics*. Clausewitz, *On War*, trans. Graham, vol. 1, book 4, chap. 4, 250; and Clausewitz, *On War*, trans. Graham, vol. 3, appendix, prop. 2–7, 243–44. Or, consider Echevarria's lament that "Clausewitz's discussions in Book IV lack the conciseness and crisp organization we find in *On War*'s introductory chapter." Echevarria, "Combat, War's only Means," 134. This can be resolved with the inclusion of *Guide to Tactics*.

[47] Christopher Coker, *Rebooting Clausewitz:* On War *in the 21st Century* (New York: Oxford University Press, 2017), 148.

clusions to be reached as open as ever to creativity
and to differing goals and points of view.[48]

Though Bassford was clearly talking about *On War*, his remarks
hold equally true for *Guide to Tactics*. In fact, *Guide to Tactics* is a
better introduction to Clausewitz for military professionals than
On War. Of course, military professionals must understand that
policy circumscribes the possibilities of military action, just as
military means serve as an instrumental extension of politics.
On War establishes the framework that fits the military into the
larger geopolitical picture. It also defines what war is. However,
such an understanding of Clausewitz will not change the day-
to-day operational or bureaucratic realities of the profession. Insights from *Guide to Tactics* very well might.

What Is the *Guide to Tactics*?

It is unclear, exactly, when and from where *Guide to Tactics*
emerged, although most scholars date the text to the period between 1810 and 1812. Schuurman, for instance, contends that the
text "may be one of the products of Clausewitz's 'Forschungen
und Bestrebungen'" (research and aspirations) during that time.
Beginning in October 1810, as Paret details, Clausewitz gave
"three weekly one-hour sessions" to the Hohenzollern dynasty's
crown prince, Friedrich Wilhelm IV; these sessions "continued
through spring, resumed in October, and ended in March 1812."[49]
During this time, Clausewitz was also teaching at the Berlin War
Academy (*Kriegsschule*).[50] In her preface to *On War*, Clausewitz's
wife and editor, Marie, explains that these circumstances—
tutoring royalty and teaching war studies—coupled with the
impetus and support from Clausewitz's mentor, Gerhard von
Scharnhorst, "gave him additional reasons for directing his research and efforts toward these matters, as well as, to set down

---

[48] Christopher Bassford, *Clausewitz in English: The Reception of Clausewitz in Britain and America, 1815–1945* (New York: Oxford University Press, 1994), 223.
[49] Paret, *Clausewitz and the State*, 193.
[50] Paret, *Clausewitz and the State*, 193.

his findings in writing."[51] Scheipers notes that "Scharnhorst imbued Clausewitz with a fiercely critical theoretical perspective and an acute sense for the relevance of history for the study of war"—both of which were essential for Clausewitz's theoretical development and written works.[52]

In his preface to the French translation, *Théorie du Combat*, Thomas Lindemann presents two possible hypotheses as to the origin of *Guide to Tactics*.[53] First, he suggests that *Guide to Tactics* may be the material Clausewitz used for the course on tactics he taught at the Berlin War Academy with Karl von Tiedemann, another Prussian officer.[54] Paret quotes a letter Clausewitz wrote to Count August Neidhardt von Gneisenau, wherein Clausewitz jests that he is teaching the product of what he referred to as the "Tiedemann-Clausewitzian factory of tactics."[55] Most scholars have analyzed this course as Clausewitz's lectures on *kleiner Krieg* (small war).[56] But Lindemann suggests that perhaps this course also included Clausewitz at his theoretical best, writing a theory of the combat—*Guide to Tactics*. This may be substantiated by Paret, according to whom Scharnhorst noted that "what Tiedemann and Clausewitz were offering their students was neither more nor less than an analysis of war as it actually is."[57] A second hypothesis proposed by Lindemann is that *Guide to Tac-*

---

[51] Clausewitz, *On War*, ed. and trans. Howard and Paret, 65–66. Compare to Charles Edward White, *The Enlightened Soldier: Scharnhorst and the Militärische Gesellschaft in Berlin, 1801–1805* (New York: Praeger, 1989).

[52] Scheipers, *On Small War*, 15.

[53] In a note, Lindemann expresses gratitude to M. Niemeyer, who was former assistant to Hahlweg and provided him with context necessary to develop these hypotheses. Thomas Lindemann, "Préface," in Carl von Clausewitz, *Théorie du Combat*, trans. Lindemann, 11n10.

[54] Lindemann, "Préface," 11.

[55] As quoted in Paret, *Clausewitz and the State*, 187.

[56] Compare to Scheipers's *On Small War*, Paret's *Clausewitz and the State*, and the translation of Clausewitz's lectures by Christopher Daase and James W. Davis, eds., *Clausewitz on Small War* (Oxford: Oxford University Press, 2015), https:doi.org/10.1093/acprof:oso/9780198737131.001.0001.

[57] Paret, *Clausewitz and the State*, 187.

tics was primarily preparatory work toward a larger undertaking, or what he calls "un grand traité"—what became *On War*.[58]

The possibility that *Guide to Tactics* could be a preparatory treatise containing seeds of Clausewitz's later works may be evidenced by its unique structure. The work is composed of 604 propositions, divided into 28 sections, describing Clausewitz's theory of combat. Strachan argues that its "succinct aphoristic style" is a precursor to the form and structure of book 1, chapter 1, of *On War*, which some scholars argue is the singular condensation of Clausewitz's thought.[59] Evaluating the notes written by Clausewitz between 1816 and 1818 and the preface to *On War*, written by his wife and editor, reveals some of the intention behind the form in which Clausewitz sought to write a theory of combat.[60]

In a note labeled by the Howard and Paret translation as "On the Genesis of his Early Manuscript on the Theory of War, Written around 1818," Clausewitz writes that he sought to "set down my conclusions" without "[following] any preliminary plan," but "in short precise, compact statements, without concern for system or formal connection."[61] Though he was explicitly referring to his thoughts on "major elements of strategy," the correspondence between the desired structure for a theory of

---

[58] Lindemann, "Préface," 11. Lindemann has a larger argument that he derives from the "Sketch of a Plan for Tactics, or the Theory of the Combat," another work collected in the Graham appendix that is missing from the Howard and Paret edition of *On War*. Clausewitz, *On War*, trans. Graham, vol. 3, appendix, 239–42. According to the sketch, part two is a "General Theory of the Combat," which is further subdivided into eight sections. Lindemann suggests that propositions 1–219 in *Guide to Tactics* represent the first seven sections, while propositions 220a–604 make up the eighth and last section. Lindemann, "Préface," 12. See also Aron, *Penser la guerre*, tome 1, 339.

[59] Strachan, *Clausewitz's* On War, 118. Compare to Diniz and Proença Júnior who argue that book 1, chapter 1, is the ultimate arbiter of Clausewitz's thought. This misses the value of considering Clausewitz's work as a whole, inconsistent though it may be. Diniz and Proença Júnior, "A Criterion for Settling Inconsistencies in Clausewitz's *On War*," 897. Strachan and Herberg-Rothe, on the other hand, contend that the work of Aron, Paret, and the Howard and Paret edition, all published during the "*annus mirabilis* for Clausewitz studies . . . privilege the first of the eight books of *On War*, and in some respects treat only the first chapter of that first book as still relevant." Strachan and Herberg-Rothe, *Clausewitz in the Twenty-First Century*, 11.

[60] Scheipers explains the value of leveraging Clausewitz's notes because "they grant us insights into the way in which Clausewitz reflected on his own intellectual development." Scheipers, *On Small War*, 123.

[61] Clausewitz, *On War*, ed. and trans. Howard and Paret, 63.

war and the observed structure of *Guide to Tactics* should be noted.[62] In particular, Clausewitz went on, the way Montesquieu, a French political philosopher best known for his *L'esprit des lois* (*The Spirit of Laws*), "dealt with his subject was vaguely in my mind."[63]

Though it is not clear whether Clausewitz was explicitly referring to *Guide to Tactics*, his observations hold: "The propositions of this book therefore, like short spans of an arch, base their axioms on the secure foundation either of experience or the nature of war as such, and are thus adequately buttressed."[64] Azar Gat explains that this formal congruence is also substantial because "when [Clausewitz] turned to write his theoretical treatise, Montesquieu's integration of the historical and empirical on the one hand with the universal on the other appears to have emerged as a model."[65] In 1818, Clausewitz also expressed a desire for "concise, aphoristic chapters."[66] Montesquieu served as the inspiration behind this style of writing as it was set forth in 1816 and desired in 1818, and—given its similarity in style (noted by Strachan), and

---

[62] Paret goes so far to note that therein "Clausewitz dealt exclusively with theory," a unique attribute, too, of *Guide to Tactics*. Paret, *Clausewitz and the State*, 360.

[63] Clausewitz, *On War*, ed. and trans. Howard and Paret, 63. Montesquieu's full name was Charles-Louis de Secondat, baron de La Brède et de Montesquieu.

[64] Clausewitz, *On War*, ed. and trans. Howard and Paret, 61.

[65] Azar Gat, *The Origins of Military Thought: From the Enlightenment to Clausewitz* (New York: Oxford University Press, 1989), 194.

[66] Clausewitz, *On War*, ed. and trans. Howard and Paret, 63.

substance (analyzed by Gat)—*Guide to Tactics* also took Montesquieu as its inspiration.[67]

Clausewitz hoped that these aphoristic compositions would serve as what he "simply wanted to call kernels."[68] Ideally, these kernels "would attract the intelligent reader by what they suggested as much as by what they expressed; in other words, I had an intelligent reader in mind, who was already familiar with the subject."[69] The short, dense propositions found in *Guide to Tactics* are kernels in Clausewitz's sense of the term. These kernels are also likely the "seeds of his later works," as Marie put it

---

[67] Both Paret and Gat allude to a lost text written by Clausewitz during his time in Koblenz. Paret, *Clausewitz and the State*, 361; and Gat, *The Origins of Military Thought*, 193. They both describe it is as a theoretical work that fits the form and content to that of *Guide to Tactics*. If this lost work were indeed *Guide to Tactics*, then it would revise the date of the text, from Strachan and Schuurman's suggestion of 1808–12, to 1816–18, when Clausewitz was in Koblenz. However, it may be that the seeds of the work germinated during the indicated time (between 1810 and 1812) but were further refined in Koblenz. This would account for Marie's direct quote of Clausewitz's note referencing Montesquieu. Moreover, the substantial congruity with Montesquieu lends more credence to this supposition than relying purely on the conjecture of when *Guide to Tactics* was written. Further research is necessary to verify or reject this hypothesis, but *Guide to Tactics* is consistent with what "Clausewitz wrote on the treatise's character" based on the notes from that time. Gat, *The Origins of Military Thought*, 193. This would need to be cross-referenced with the recent work by Paul Donker, who has worked on reconstructing *Vom Kriege*'s development. Compare Paul Donker, "The Evolution of Clausewitz's *Vom Kriege*: A Reconstruction on the Basis of the Earlier Versions of His Masterpiece," trans. Paul Donker and Christopher Bassford, ClausewitzStudies.org (website), 2019. Donker does not include *Guide to Tactics* in the developmental history. However, Anders Palmgren cites a letter written in August 1816, from Gneisenau, one of Clausewitz's closest friends, wherein he describes how Clausewitz was to write a *Gefectlehre*. Anders Palmgren, "Visions of Strategy: Following Clausewitz's Train of Thought" (PhD diss., National Defense University, 2014), 169. Palmgren notes the connection to *Guide to Tactics* and briefly observes that "this also suggests the starting point for *Vom Kriege*." Palmgren, "Visions of Strategy," 170. Finally, Bruno Colson's biography of Clausewitz situates the text between 1816 and 1818. Colson similarly describes these propositions as "*graines*," which connects again to the seeds referenced in the notes. Bruno Colson, *Clausewitz* (Paris: Perrin, 2016), 466. His evidence is corroborated by personal correspondence with the scholar Andreas Herberg-Rothe who notes, contrary to Hahlweg, that this text is likely from 1816–18 and not 1809–12. Colson, *Clausewitz*, 311, 447n142.

[68] Clausewitz, *On War*, ed. and trans. Howard and Paret, 63.

[69] Clausewitz, *On War*, ed. and trans. Howard and Paret, 63.

in her preface to *On War*.[70] Clausewitz extended and transcended the theory of the combat that underwrote *Guide to Tactics* to develop the theory of war that became *On War*. The necessary connection between tactics and strategy would warrant a theory of combat as important, if not imperative, to "major elements of strategy," if for no other reason than the fact that it is the material of which strategy is composed.[71] However, *On War*'s success has overshadowed the kernels of thought, the *Guide to Tactics*, out of which it was built.

Publication and Translations of *On War*

If, as we have seen, *Guide to Tactics* significantly furthers our understanding of *On War*, and contains seeds of Clausewitz's future works, why has it been nearly ignored by scholarly attention for decades? While Thomas Lindemann (supported by a combined effort between the French think tank, L'Institut de Stratégie Comparée, and the French military academy, L'École militaire de Saint-Cyr) translated the German text into a stand-alone French text, *Théorie du Combat*, published in 1998, the text is mentioned in very few English scholarly works, and then only in passing. John E. Tashjean, in reviewing Hahlweg's 1980 edition of *Vom Kriege*, notes that the "substantial appendices" include "writings by Clausewitz [that] document his tactical and pedagogical ideas."[72] In *Penser la guerre*, Aron abstains from engaging with the

---

[70] Clausewitz, *On War*, ed. and trans. Howard and Paret, 66. Compare to Aron, *Penser la guerre*, tome 1, 271. However, there is ambiguity as to which seed-work she refers, even as she describes their germination from "an essay with which he concluded the instruction of His Royal Highness the Crown Prince in 1812." This is likely a reference to *Guide to Tactics*. What lends credence to the suggestion that Marie is referring to *Guide to Tactics*, rather than to the conclusion of *Principles of War*, is that she includes Clausewitz's note written around 1818, described above. This is less obvious in the Howard and Paret edition, since they extract the cited note from Marie's preface. Hahlweg's *Vom Kriege* maintains the continuity of Marie's thought. Clausewitz, *Vom Kreige*, 175. Given the note's reference to Montesquieu and his style, whose influence is evident in *Guide to Tactics*, it seems more likely that Marie is referring to *Guide to Tactics* rather than *Principles of War*. This observation is also made by Lindemann. Lindemann, "Préface," 11.

[71] Clausewitz, *On War*, ed. and trans. Howard and Paret, 63.

[72] John E. Tashjean et al., "Book Reviews," *Journal of Strategic Studies* 4, no. 2 (1981): 210, https://doi.org/10.1080/01402398108437078. Although this is a review of the 1980 edition, the *Leitfaden* was included in the 1952 edition from which Howard and Paret derived their version of *On War*.

text, noting, however, that at an epistemological and conceptual level *Guide to Tactics* is methodologically consistent with *On War*.[73] Strachan sees it as a step beyond "elementary tactics of the sergeant" toward the "higher tactics" that are found in book 4 of *On War*.[74] Schuurman leverages *Guide to Tactics* to highlight the continuity in Clausewitz's thought concerning adversarial interaction, relationships between wholes and parts, and the nature of military forces.[75] Andreas Herberg-Rothe sees this "very early text" as one of the few instances in which polarity appears.[76] These references aside, *Guide to Tactics* has languished in relative obscurity among English scholars of Clausewitz.

The reasons for this oversight are based in large part on the publication history of, somewhat unexpectedly, *Vom Kriege* and its English translations. After Clausewitz died of cholera in 1831, Marie von Clausewitz edited his collected works, and published them with the help of Major Franz August O'Etzel, a colleague of Clausewitz's, and her brother, Lieutenant General Friedrich Wilhelm von Brühl.[77] Her husband had, she noted, foretold it: "*You* shall publish it."[78] The collection, entitled *Hinterlassene Werke* (*Posthumous Works*), eventually contained 10 volumes. The first three amounted to *Vom Kriege* and were published between 1832 and 1834.[79] In her preface, Marie makes it clear that the "literary remains are published . . . exactly as they were found, without

---

[73] Aron, *Penser la guerre*, tome 1, 30. Strikingly, Aron continues, "Ce texte, entièrement négligé par les lecteurs français avant 1914, aurait évité bien des erreurs." (This text, entirely neglected by French readers before 1914, would have avoided many errors.) Aron includes a short analysis using *Guide to Tactics* to support the differentiation between the defense, which has a negative object, and the attack, which has a positive object; both still have victory as their ultimate goal. Aron, *Penser la guerre*, tome 1, 271. In one of his extended notes, Aron observes that the sense of polarity found in *Guide to Tactics* is more inclusive than that which is found in *On War*. Aron, *Penser la guerre*, tome 1, 407n17.
[74] Strachan, *Clausewitz's* On War, 118. Some anachronisms persist and the annotations that follow, the author hopes, will help to locate these deviations due to changes in the character of warfare or in the evolution of Clausewitz's thought.
[75] Schuurman, "War as a System," 928.
[76] Andreas Herberg-Rothe, *Clausewitz's Puzzle: The Political Theory of War* (New York: Oxford University Press, 2007), 122, https://doi.org/10.1093/acprof:osof /9780199202690.001.0001.
[77] Strachan, *Clausewitz's* On War, 69.
[78] Clausewitz, *On War*, ed. and trans. Howard and Paret, 65.
[79] Strachan, *Clausewitz's* On War, 69.

one word being added or deleted."[80] After Marie died in 1836, the 10th and final volume was published.[81] Without amendments, the first edition of *Vom Kriege* contained numerous errors and misprints, and more extensive "contradictions and obscurities" beyond those one might expect to be levied against any incomplete text published posthumously.[82] In the second edition, begun in 1853 and completed in 1857, Marie's brother "introduced several hundred changes, far beyond fixing grammatical and print errors or modernization of the language."[83] Werner Hahlweg, editor of the 16th edition of *Vom Kriege*, discovered Brühl's textual interventions.[84] In 1952, almost a century after their introduction, Hahlweg reverted the text back to that which was found in the original three volumes that comprised *Vom Kriege*.[85] The textual sins Brühl introduced, primarily to book 8, chapter 6B, made it seem that "the military should have a greater say in state policy making."[86] Brühl's revised text was the standard edition of *Vom Kriege* in German and English until Hahlweg's corrections were made after World War II.[87]

The contentious legacy of the German editions helped to establish the primacy of the 1976 Howard and Paret edition and translation. Unlike the previous two English translations, one by British colonel James John Graham in 1873 and the other by

---

[80] Clausewitz, *On War*, ed. and trans. Howard and Paret, 65.

[81] Strachan, *Clausewitz's* On War, 69.

[82] Strachan, *Clausewitz's* On War, 69.

[83] Strachan, *Clausewitz's* On War, 69–70; and Vanya Eftimova Bellinger, *Marie von Clausewtiz: The Woman Behind the Making of* On War (New York: Oxford University Press, 2016), 226.

[84] Honig, "Interpreting Clausewitz," 578n1.

[85] Hew Strachan and Andreas Herberg-Rothe "Introduction," *Clausewitz in the Twenty-First Century*, 13.

[86] Honig, "Interpreting Clausewitz," 578n1. Strachan provides an additional sobering point: "The significance of this change is perhaps less important than others made by Brühl and O'Etzel, which unlike this one we cannot now trace because they were made to the first edition." Strachan, *Clausewitz's* On War, 70. But this comment is at odds with Marie's note. There is an irony too: Brühl, a military officer, intervened to modify a text that had explicitly subordinated the military to politics and policy; he rejected the supposition and deliberately reversed the text (as if such a textual change could revise a theory revealed from considering the text as a whole), to reposition and expand the influence of the military. Compare to Clausewitz, *On War*, trans. Howard and Paret, book 8, chap. 6, 608n1.

[87] Bellinger, *Marie von Clausewtiz*, 226.

German expatriate Otto Jolle Matthijs Jolles in 1943, Howard and Paret's edition was based on Hahlweg's 1952 edition that had corrected Brühl's intrusion and returned *Vom Kriege* to the originally published vestal text. Previously, the most popular English translation had been Graham's, which was based on the German third edition.[88]

The Howard and Paret translation of *On War* is now considered "the norm amongst scholars" and should be recognized for helping to ignite Clausewitzian studies in the United States by rekindling a "Clausewitzian Renaissance."[89] Strachan and Herberg-Rothe, in their introduction to *Clausewitz in the Twenty-First Century*, claim that "it is not too much to say that when many English-language scholars discuss *On War*, they are in reality discussing Howard and Paret's interpretation of it."[90] Jan Willem Honig's essay, "Clausewitz's *On War*: Problems of Text and Translation," notes, too, that once Howard and Paret's translation and edition emerged, "the English translation of *On War* also no longer appears to be an issue." He continues:

> the most recent [translation], undertaken by Michael Howard and Peter Paret (based on a partial draft by Angus Malcolm), is overwhelmingly considered the best. This translation has received very little criticism. It has become the standard text, not only in the English-speaking world, but it is even given preferential treatment by students in countries where one might have expected the original German to remain accessible. This brings out readability as one of its key advantages over the older translations (and even the original German!).[91]

---

[88] Bassford, *Clausewitz in English*, 82; and Jan Willem Hong, "Introduction to the New Edition," Carl von Clausewitz, *On War*, trans. Col J. J. Graham (New York: Barnes and Noble, 2004), xxiv–xv.

[89] Cormier, *War as Paradox*, xvn; and Honig, "Clausewitz's *On War*," 73.

[90] Strachan and Herberg-Rothe, "Introduction," *Clausewitz in the Twenty-First Century*, 13.

[91] Honig, "Clausewitz's *On War*," 58. This is corroborated by Strachan, who notes, "The Princeton edition of *On War* has proved far more successful than the German original ever was." Strachan, *Clausewitz's* On War, 1.

What is missing, however, from this edition, is the appendix that was included in the Graham translation, the Hahlweg editions, and the older German editions.[92]

Insidiously, though unintentionally, and certainly not unilaterally, the primacy of the now-ubiquitous English translation of *On War* by Howard and Paret has reinforced the obscurity of *Guide to Tactics*. This is a criticism of the Howard and Paret edition separate and distinct from critiques about their translation.[93] Our concern here is that although Howard and Paret based their translation on Hahlweg's 1952 edition, in which *Guide to Tactics* was found, the text is not included in their edition.[94]

For our purposes, we have used the Graham translation of *Guide to Tactics* republished by British colonel Frederic Natusch Maude in 1908 (to much greater success, in fact, than Graham's original publishing run).[95] This edition was reprinted in 1918. There are limitations to this translation, just as there are limitations to any Clausewitz translation, including the reigning Howard and Paret edition of *On War*. Hans Rothfels, whose 1943 essay in Edward Mead Earle's *Makers of Modern Strategy* introduced Clausewitz to scholars like Bernard Brodie and Michael Howard, explains, referring to *On War*, that the Graham translation "is by no means free from misunderstandings and plain errors."[96] Other scholars, like Tashjean, stridently repudiate "the textual atrocities committed in decades past by Colonels Graham and Maude" in favor of the then-newly published Howard

[92] Bassford, *Clausewitz in English*, 58; and Honig, "Clausewitz's *On War*," 58n7.

[93] Many scholars have critiqued Howard and Paret on this particular point. Sibylle Scheipers notes, "In this intellectual climate i.e., the era of nuclear deterrence, Michael Howard and Peter Paret published a new translation of *On War* . . . which is thoroughly influenced by the reading of Clausewitz as the proponent of war as an instrument of policy." Scheipers, *On Small War*, 7. See also Honig, "Clausewitz's *On War*," 70.

[94] John E. Tashjean, "The Transatlantic Clausewitz, 1952–1982," *Naval War College Review* 35, no. 6 (November–December 1982): 70. Herberg-Rothe explicitly notes in a footnote how the *Leitfaden* was "not translated in the Howard and Paret edition." Herberg-Rothe, *Clausewitz's Puzzle*, 179n169.

[95] Bassford, *Clausewitz in English*, 57, 74, 81.

[96] Bassford, *Clausewitz in English*, 185. Here, Howard is quoted explaining that Rothfels's piece was "the first serious study of Clausewitz that many of us ever saw." Hans Rothfels, "Clausewitz," in *Makers of Modern Strategy: Military Thought from Machiavelli to Hitler*, ed. Edward Mead Earle (Princeton, NJ: Princeton University Press, 1943), 95n9. Those plain "errors" would have included the deliberate adjustment by Brühl noted earlier.

and Paret translation (again, only of *On War*).[97] W. B. Gallie offers
a different, balanced view. He values Graham's edition because
it "has been reprinted no fewer than nine times, which testified
to its readability."[98] Still, he caveats, Graham's translation fails
to include "the smooth style of the original and in places it could
easily mislead the modern reader."[99] Given that there is neither
a Jolles nor a Howard and Paret translation of *Guide to Tactics*,
we follow Jon T. Sumida, who claims that the "standard English
translation" can be considered "sufficient."[100] Beyond that sufficiency, however, many scholars also argue in support of the Graham translation. Cormier notes that while Graham's edition is
"not always the most practical for everyday use, it is more help-
ful in uncovering word choices and concepts that Clausewitz
borrowed from philosophical literature."[101] Coker advises that
Graham's "version is much more faithful to the German even if
it is not as fluent as the Howard/Paret version."[102] In the introduction to the modern Graham edition, Honig explains that this
translation

> possesses a number of important strengths. In a
> general sense, its age makes it nearest in time to the
> original and thus it most closely approximates the
> intellectual climate of Clausewitz's world. The trans-
> lation is also faithful to the original in the sense of
> being literal and consistent in its rendering of Clause-
> witz's terminology. As a result, the structure and co-
> herence of Clausewitz's thought come through more

[97] Tashjean, "The Transatlantic Clausewitz, 1952–1982," 76.

[98] W. B. Gallie, *Philosophers of Peace and War: Kant, Clausewitz, Marx, Engels and Tolstoy* (Cambridge, UK: Cambridge University Press, 1978), 143, https://doi.org/10.1017/CBO 9780511558450.

[99] Gallie, *Philosophers of Peace and War*, 143.

[100] Jon T. Sumida, "The Clausewitz Problem," *Army History*, no. 73 (Fall 2009): 17. Sumida is not clear about which English translations count as sufficient. In *Decoding Clausewitz*, he includes both Howard/Paret and Graham's translations in his bibliography. He fails, again, to include the necessary specificity for his claim. Sumida, *Decoding Clausewitz*, 7. Despite this ambiguity, Graham's translation, like Jolles's and Howard/Paret's, is suffi-cient to grasp the overall tenor of Clausewitz's thoughts.

[101] Cormier, *War as Paradox*, xvn.

[102] Coker, *Rebooting Clausewitz*, 159.

clearly than tends to be the case with the more modern translations.[103]

Given that *Guide to Tactics* can be found in English only in Graham's translation, its literal literary isolation hints at why it has been underexplored. It has never before been published in English as a stand-alone text.

Principles of War—What *Guide to Tactics* Is Not

There is a second reason that *Guide to Tactics* has remained little known: its frequent confusion with another Clausewitzian work of the time, *Principles of War*. *Principles of War*, often claimed, erroneously, to be an abridgment of *On War*, is a text summarizing the instruction that Clausewitz gave to the young members of the Hohenzollern dynasty.[104] It is obsequious, short, prescriptive, and legible—all characteristics that Clausewitz desperately sought to dissociate himself from in *On War*.

In the Graham translation of *On War*, multiple texts, including *Guide to Tactics* and *Principles of War*, are compiled under the appendix title "Summary of the Instruction Given by the Author to His Royal Highness the Crown Prince in the Years 1810, 1811, and 1812."[105] All too often, it is unclear which texts are included when scholars (e.g., Christopher Bassford) refer to Clausewitz's "Instructions for the Crown Prince." *Principles of War* is actually a misnomer, since it refers to a particular translation by Hans W. Gatzke. Gatzke's *Principles of War* was published in 1942 based on a 1936 German edition edited by *Luftwaffe* general Friedrich von Cochenhausen, and it is equivalent only to a portion of the collected texts found in the Graham appendix.[106] Within the ap-

---

[103] Honig, "Introduction to the New Edition," xxiv–xv.
[104] Bassford, *Clausewitz in English*, 221.
[105] Clausewitz, *On War*, trans. Graham, vol. 3, appendix, 178–337. Included in the appendix are five texts: "Scheme which Was Laid before General Von Gaudy"; "The Most Important Principles of the Art of War to Complete My Course of Instruction of His Royal Highness the Crown Prince," which Hans Gatzke, in 1942, separately translated as *Principles of War*; "On the Organic Division of Armed Forces"; "Sketch of a Plan for Tactics, or the Theory of the Combat"; and "Guide to Tactics, or the Theory of the Combat," which is republished herein.
[106] Bassford, *Clausewitz in English*, 264n17.

pendix, the text is known as "The Most Important Principles of the Art of War to Complete My Course of Instruction of His Royal Highness the Crown Prince."[107] Yet Bassford, who traces the intellectual history of Clausewitz's *On War* in English, conflates *Principles of War* with the larger collection of texts found in the Graham appendix. For instance, he notes how "a new translation of the 'Instruction for the Crown Prince' appeared in the United States in 1942," although, puzzlingly, he is aware that "Gatzke's translation was not nearly so complete as the Graham version."[108] This is a contradiction.[109] In other words, Bassford refers to the "Instructions for the Crown Prince" as another title for Gatzke's *Principles of War*, and yet also considers the title inclusive of all the texts in the Graham appendix. In so doing, he would include *Guide to Tactics*, which is *not* found within *Principles of War*. This referential confusion is suggestive, however, of how *Guide to Tactics* has remained relatively unknown and superseded by—or mistaken for—the toadying *Principles of War*.

Principles of War has not aged well because it was written for the crown prince's personal consumption. Unlike the more theoretical scope of *Guide to Tactics*, *Principles of War* delineates specific tactics, or "arrangement of military force," for the crown prince to defend Prussia against Napoleon, and it reads as anachronistic because it is; it specifies, albeit generally, how the crown prince should fight. Just prior to renouncing his Prussian commission, in 1812, to fight against Napoleon with the Russians, Clausewitz compiled a collection of the tutoring he had conducted during the preceding two years.[110] This became known, variously, as "the most important principles for the conduct of war," "Instructions for the Crown Prince," and often now *Prin-*

---

[107] Clausewitz, *On War*, trans. Graham, vol. 3, appendix, 182–229.

[108] Bassford, *Clausewitz in English*, 122. Bassford contends that Gatzke did not know of Graham's translation. Bassford, *Clausewitz in English*, 181.

[109] In a note, Bassford cites from *Guide to Tactics*, referencing the sections "Relation between the Magnitude and Certainty of the Result" and "Relation between the Magnitude of the Result and the Price" to support a connection to the requirement for boldness found in *On War*, particularly book 3, chapter 6. He cites it as "Instruction for the Crown Prince." Bassford, *Clausewitz in English*, 246n39.

[110] Strachan, *Clausewitz's* On War, 68.

ciples of War.[111] Bassford underscores that it "had been written for the edification of a child."[112] Paret details that not only was the crown prince 15 when he started his tutorial in 1810, but that in 1811, his younger brother William and the 14-year-old Prince Frederick of the Netherlands also joined the lessons, compelling Clausewitz into "presenting his thoughts in the simplest terms possible."[113] Paret observes, "It would have amused Clausewitz with his scorn for dogma that his words to a seventeen-year-old boy became the precedent for the conventional checklists of rules and laws by which military academies and staff schools in the 20th century try to make war comprehensible and manageable to their pupils."[114]

Although *Principles of War* is better known than *Guide to Tactics*, it is less useful. To begin with, the Graham appendix opens with Clausewitz's "Scheme which Was Laid before General [Friedrich Wilhelm] Von Gaudy," in which he explains that in *Principles of War* he sought "to avoid diffuseness, or taxing the Prince's faculties too much."[115] This choice neutered many of the qualities that made Clausewitz's work unique—the longevity and originality of his thought, and what Hans Rothfels described as his ability to conduct "analysis of the structural elements of war with an undogmatic elasticity and a great power of discrimination."[116] These strengths of Clausewitz are in direct conflict with the "didactic form" in which *Principles of War* is presented and which, importantly, does not restrict *Guide to Tactics*.[117]

---

[111] Strachan, *Clausewitz's* On War, 68; and Bassford, *Clausewitz in English*, 120.

[112] Bassford, *Clausewitz in English*, 120. It is worth tempering this with his further observation that "although this is sometimes denigrated as being mere instructions for a child, it is useful to remember that the child was the heir apparent of the Hohenzollern dynasty. That family demanded a high degree of military professionalism from its sons, as well it might, since the fortunes of Prussia were uniquely dependent on the military talents of its ruling house." Bassford, *Clausewitz in English*, 88.

[113] Paret, *Clausewitz and the State*, 193–94.

[114] Paret, *Clausewitz and the State*, 196n65. This is further corroborated by Bassford: "At the doctrinal level, it is easy to find attempts to use Clausewitz's writings, especially his 'Instruction for the Crown Prince', as the basis for lists of 'principles' and for tactical prescriptions of all kinds. The 'Instruction' was readily available in English after 1873." Bassford, *Clausewitz in English*, 107.

[115] Clausewitz, *On War*, trans. Graham, vol. 3, appendix, 178.

[116] Rothfels, "Clausewitz," 101.

[117] Gat, *The Origins of Military Thought*, 193.

In fact, Vanya Bellinger's observation that *On War* "was written in a realist philosophical language without the heroic pathos or emphatic talk of manly honor" can be equally well applied to *Guide to Tactics*.[118] But such pathos is exactly how Clausewitz concludes *Principles of War*, after invoking Caesar, Hannibal, and Frederick the Great, in "a paean on the qualities of self-confidence and heroism."[119] "Be bold and astute in your designs," Clausewitz petitions the crown prince, "firm and preserving in executing them, determined to find a glorious end, and destiny will press on your youthful brow a radiant crown—fit emblem of a prince, the rays of which will carry your image into the bosom of your latest descendants."[120] Though the text is ingratiating in tone, there are still concepts and ideas that carry over into *On War*—but not to the extent that and in the way in which, as we have seen, *Guide to Tactics* does.

Nevertheless, *Principles of War* has often, and erroneously, been considered a summary of, or equivalent to, *On War*. For instance, in a 1905 article, Bassford noted how Lieutenant Colonel Charles à Court Repington referred to "Instruction for the Crown Prince" when commending Clausewitz: "Britons did not make much distinction, since the 'Instruction' appeared as an appendix in the Graham translation."[121] Additionally, Bassford observes, when Gatzke's translation of *Principles of War* was published, "reviewers were enthusiastic and saw *Principles of War* as simply a shorter, more readable version of *On War*."[122] In summarizing its content, Paret writes that the essay "offers a synthesis of Clausewitz's ideas on tactics, strategy, and the relationship between study and reality, reduced to simple declarative sentences and brief numbered paragraphs, which, as he wrote in an

---

[118] Bellinger, *Marie von Clausewtiz*, 191.

[119] Paret, *Clausewitz and the State*, 199.

[120] Clausewitz, *On War*, trans. Graham, vol. 3, appendix, 229.

[121] Bassford, *Clausewitz in English*, 74. Repington was incorrectly identified as Thomas.

[122] Bassford, *Clausewitz in English*, 181. Bassford is careful to distinguish how the German expatriates, such as Alfred Vagts—who reviewed Gatzke's *Principles of War* for the *New Republic* and for whom the American Clausewitzian Renaissance owes a debt of gratitude—disagreed with this substitution.

introductory note, were designed to stimulate thought rather than offer a complete body of instruction."[123] Though that may sound like the content of *On War* (though not its form), *Principles of War* is still, as Bassford describes, only "a primitive precursor" found "in appropriately simplified form."[124]

Although *Principles of War* has clear intellectual currents that link it to *On War*, *Guide to Tactics*, as we have seen, is far more connected to Clausewitz's most famous work. What differentiates *Principles of War* and *Guide to Tactics* from *On War* is their continuity with it. *Principles of War* contains concepts, like friction, that Clausewitz makes use of (for instance, in book 1, chapter 7), whereas *Guide to Tactics* is deeply embedded in the underlying theoretical structure from which *On War* emerged.[125]

In the introduction to his translation, Graham observed that Clausewitz's "fame rests most upon the three volumes forming his treatise on 'War'."[126] This fame would have included both what we know now as *On War* and *Principles of War*, as well as *Guide to Tactics*. But with the primacy of the Howard and Paret edition of *On War*, *Guide to Tactics* has receded from view. It is now time to restore *Guide to Tactics* to its former attraction and grant it, too, the renown it deserves.

A Note on How to Read the Text

As indicated, *Guide to Tactics* is a theoretical text. Like *On War*, it is not prescriptive. There are no definitive answers to what one should or should not do in combat. Instead, it serves as a guide to how to think about combat. The task of understanding what it means to exercise violence in the service of political ends is an unyielding, continuous process. Reading *Guide to Tactics* is a part of that activity. It should be hard but rewarding, like finishing a field exercise. And like a field exercise, the point is the time spent in exertion: What do you learn about yourself and your fellow Marines in the process?

---

[123] Paret, *Clausewitz and the State*, 194.

[124] Bassford, *Clausewitz in English*, 10.

[125] Strachan, *Clausewitz's* On War, 118.

[126] Clausewitz, *On War*, trans. Graham, vol. 1, xxxvii.

Reading *Guide to Tactics* can be considered a mental field exercise, where time spent with this text should be well-earned. Write in the margins. Dog-ear sections. Question its wisdom. Apply what makes sense. Share your doubts. Above all, begin a dialogue.

The structure that follows places the original text on one page and the annotations on the facing page. There is a limited number of annotations and a lot of white space. This is intentional. The included annotations are meant to serve as a guide with which to make your own. Use the lined pages to note your thoughts. Draw sketches of Clausewitz's thought experiments. Compare his theory with your recent experience. Explore a historical example, or a fictional one. Evaluate a video game or a wargame based on this theory. Chart your own course. There is no right way to read this text. Make it useful by making it yours.

Finally, readers may note that throughout the source text, Clausewitz uses the pronouns *he*, *him*, or *his* to refer to a theoretical leader, soldier, etc., as was the convention at the time. That leader should be read to include all Marines.

Olivia A. Garard

ANNOTATED *GUIDE TO TACTICS, OR THE THEORY OF THE COMBAT*[1]

I.—: GENERAL THEORY OF THE COMBAT

Object of the Combat[2]
(1) What is the object of the combat?

    (a) Destruction of the enemy's armed forces.

    (b) To gain possession of some object.[3]

    (c) Merely victory for the credit of our arms.

    (d) Two of these objects, or all three taken together.

Theory of Victory
(2) Any of these four objects can only be obtained by a *victory*.

(3) Victory is the retirement of the enemy from the field of battle.[4]

(4) The enemy is moved to this:[5]

    (a) If his loss is excessive,

      (i) and he therefore fears he will be overpowered,

      (ii) or finds that the object will cost him too much.

    (b) If the formation of his Army, consequently the efficiency of the whole, is too much shaken.

    (c) If he begins to get on disadvantageous ground, and therefore has to fear excessive loss if he continues the combat. (In this is therefore included the loss of the position.)

    (d) If the form of the order of battle is attended with too great disadvantages.

    (e) If he is taken by surprise in any way, or suddenly attacked, and therefore has not time to make suitable dispositions to give his measures their proper development.

[1] The source of the text in this annotated work is Gen Carl von Clausewitz, *On War*, trans. Col J. J. Graham (London: Kegan Paul, Trench, Trubner, 1918), vol. 3, 243–337. All future references to *On War* in this section refer to this edition. The punctuation, capitalization, and British spellings of this translation have been retained throughout this work. Readers may note that throughout the source text, Clausewitz uses the pronouns *he*, *him*, or *his* to refer to a theoretical leader, soldier, etc., as was the convention at the time. In this section, the original text is on the left pages and critical annotations are on the right. Annotations are intentionally limited and should serve as a guide for making your own notes about the text.

[2] The object of the combat is means to impose will. The object of war is to compel an enemy to do your will. *Warfighting*, Marine Corps Doctrinal Publication 1 (MCDP 1) (Washington, DC: Headquarters Marine Corps, 1997), 4.

[3] Possession of an object can be terrain, for example, a hill, or it can be a population or resources. *Credit* speaks to the informational value of tactical action.

[4] The battlefield is amorphous, multidimensional, including various domains.

[5] These are all mental states: "fears," "finds," "is shaken," "perceives," and "is surprised."

(f) If he perceives that his opponent is too superior to him in numbers.

(g) If he perceives that his opponent has too great a superiority in moral forces.

(5) In all these cases a Commander may give up the combat, because he has no hope of matters taking a favourable turn, and has to apprehend that his situation will become still worse than it is at present.[6]

(6) Except upon one of these grounds a retreat is not justifiable, and, therefore, cannot be the decision of the General or Commander.

(7) But a retreat can be made in point of fact without his will.[7]

(a) If the troops, from want of courage or of good will, give way.

(b) If a panic drives them off.

(8) Under these circumstances, the victory may be conceded to the enemy against the will of the Commander, and even when the results springing from the other relations enumerated from *a* to *f* incline in our favour.

(9) This case can and must often happen with small bodies of troops. The short duration of the whole act often hardly leaves the Commander time to form a resolution.[8]

(10a) But with large masses, such a case can only occur with parts of the force, not easily with the whole. Should, however, several parts yield the victory thus easily to the enemy, a disadvantageous result for the whole may ensue in those respects noted from *a* to *e*, and thus the Commander may be compelled to resolve upon withdrawing from the field.

(10b) With a large mass, the disadvantageous relations specified under *a, b, c* and *d*, do not exhibit themselves to the Commander

[6] This creates a situation where the enemy believes that they have "no hope of matters taking a favourable turn." See also *Warfighting*, 73.

[7] This is not just a function of the commander's perception but also that of the troops at their command.

[8] The smaller the scale, the faster these effects permeate the whole.

in the arithmetical sum of all partial disadvantages which have taken place, for the general view is never so complete, but they show themselves where, being compressed into a narrow compass, they form an imposing whole. This may be the case either with the principal body, or an important part of that body. The resolution then is decided by this predominant feature of the whole act.[9]

(11) Lastly, the Commander may be prompted to give up the combat, and therefore to retreat for reasons which do not lie in the combat, but which may be regarded as foreign to it, such as intelligence, which does away with the object, or materially alters the strategic relations. This would be a breaking off of the combat, and does not belong to this place, because it is a strategic, not a tactical, act.[10]

(12) The giving up of the combat is, therefore, an acknowledgment of the temporary superiority of our opponent, let it be either physically or morally, *and a yielding to his will.* In that consists the first moral force of victory.

(13) As we can only give up the combat by leaving the field of battle, therefore the retirement from the field is *the sign of this acknowledgment, the lowering of our flag* as it were.

(14) *But the sign of victory* still decides nothing as to its greatness, importance, or splendour. These three things often coincide, but are by no means identical.

(15) The greatness of a victory depends on the greatness of the masses over which it has been gained, as well as on the greatness of the trophies. Captured guns, prisoners, baggage taken, killed, wounded, belong to this. Therefore, over a small body of troops no great victory can be gained.[11]

[9] There is a scale, intensity, and concentration of effects.

[10] Sometimes strategy reaches down and demands tactical changes that within the immediate tactical situation may not make sense (or be actively counterintuitive) but that from the 30,000-foot level are required. This is good and necessary.

[11] The greatness of victory is how it relates to strategy, which, in this case, means that beating a large number of troops has a greater effect than beating a smaller number. This emphasis on numbers, as mass, is a product of the Napoleonic era.

(16) The importance of the victory depends on the importance of the object which it secures to us. The conquest of an important position may make an insignificant victory very important.

(17) The splendour of a victory depends on the proportion which the number of trophies bears to the strength of the victorious Army.[12]

(18) There are therefore victories of different kinds and of many different degrees. Strictly speaking, there can be no combat without a decision, consequently without a victory; but the ordinary use of language and the nature of the thing require that we should only consider those results of combats as victories which have been preceded by very considerable efforts.[13]

(19) If the enemy contents himself with doing just sufficient to ascertain our designs, and as soon as he has found them out gives way, we cannot call that a victory; if he does more than that, it can only be done with a view to becoming conqueror in reality, and, therefore, in that case, if he gives up the combat, he is to be considered as conquered.

(20) As a combat can only cease by one or other or both of the parties who have been in contact retiring partially, therefore it can never be said, properly speaking, that both parties have kept the field. In so far, however, as the nature of the thing and the ordinary use of language require us to understand by the term battlefield the position of the principal masses of the contending Armies, and because the first consequences of victory only commence with the retreat of the *principal masses*, therefore there may be battles which remain quite indecisive.[14]

The Combat is the Means of gaining a Victory
(21) The means to obtain victory is the combat. As the points specified in No. 4 from *a* to *g* establish the victory, therefore also the combat is directed on those points as its immediate objects.[15]

[12] It is not a one-to-one effect; there is a relativity to it.

[13] This is more a product of the requirement to marshal forces to achieve a big decision (strategic effect). All combats have some sort of decision, but not all have the same degree of decision.

[14] A battlefield is the position of the principal masses of contending forces. This is inclusive of terrain, but not exclusive of cyber, the electromagnetic spectrum, space, or information. This is the battlespace.

[15] (4) The enemy is moved to [evacuate the battlefield]:
    (a) If his loss is excessive,
        (i) . . . fears he will be overpowered,
        (ii) . . . the object will cost him too much.
    (b) . . . formation of his Army . . . is too much shaken.
    (c) . . . fear excessive loss if he continues the combat.
    (d) . . . order of battle is attended with too great disadvantages.
    (e) . . . taken by surprise . . . or suddenly attacked.
    (f) . . . perceives that his opponent is too superior.
    (g) . . . opponent has too great a superiority in moral forces.
As found on p. 30.

(22) We must now make ourselves acquainted with the combat in its different phases.

What is an Independent Combat?

(23) In reality, every combat may be separated into as many single combats as there are combatants. But the individual only appears as a separate item when he fights singly, that is, independently.

(24) From single combats the units ascend to fresh units coordinately with the ascending scale of subdivisions of command.

(25) These units are bound together through the object and the plan, still not so closely that the members do not retain a certain degree of independence. This always becomes greater the higher the rank of the units. How this gain of independence on the part of the members takes place we shall show afterwards.

(26) Thus every total combat consists of a great number of separate combats in descending order of members (No. 97, &c.) down to the lowest member acting independently.[16]

(27) But a total combat consists also of separate combats following one another in succession.

(28) All separate combats we call partial combats, and the whole of them a total combat; but we connect the conception of a whole combat with the supposed condition of a personal command, and therefore only that belongs to *one* combat which is directed by *one* will. (In cordon positions the limits between the two can never be defined.)[17]

(29) What has been said here on the theory of combat relates to the total combat, as well as to the partial combat.

.

[16] These members could be considered at the level of the fireteam, the platoon, the squadron, the division, or even the Joint Force. Editorial note: the abbreviation &c. is a precursor to the modern *etc.*, which is an abbreviation of the Latin *et cetera*, meaning "and the other things."

[17] See Clausewitz, *On War*, vol. 2, book 6, chap. 22, 297–301.

Principles of the Combat[18]

(30) Every fight is an expression of hostility, which passes into combat instinctively.

(31) This instinct to attack and destroy the enemy is the real element of War.

(32) Even amongst the most savage tribes, this impulse to hostility is not pure instinct alone; the reflecting intelligence supervenes, aimless instinct becomes an act with a purpose.[19]

(33) In this manner the feelings are made submissive to the understanding.

(34) But we can never consider them as completely eliminated, and the pure object of reason substituted in their place; for if they were swallowed up in the object of reason, they would come to life again spontaneously in the heat of the combat.

(35) As our Wars are not utterances of the hostility of individuals opposed to individuals, so the combat seems to be divested of all real hostility, and therefore to be a purely reasonable action.

(36) But it is not so by any means. Partly there is never wanting a collective hatred between the parties, which then manifests itself more or less effectively in the individual, so that from hating and warring against a party, he hates and wars against the individual man as well; partly in the course of a combat itself a real feeling of hostility is kindled more or less in the individuals engaged.

(37) Desire of fame, ambition, self-interest, and *esprit de corps*, along with other feelings, take the place of hostility when that does not exist.

(38) Therefore, the mere will of the Commander, the mere prescribed object, is seldom or never the sole motive of action in the

[18] These ideas are most clearly described in Clausewitz's trinity, found in Clausewitz, *On War*, vol. 1, book 1, chap. 1, 25–26.

[19] Aimless hostility is not the point of combat. It does not serve strategy and is likely in violation of the rules of engagement or the warrior ethos.

combatants; instead of that, a very notable portion of the emotional forces will always be in activity.[20]

(39) This activity is increased by the circumstance of the combat moving in the region of danger, in which all emotional forces have greater weight.

(40) But even the intelligence which guides the combat can never be a power purely of the understanding, and, therefore, the combat can never be a subject of pure calculation.[21]

  (a) Because it is the collision of living physical and moral forces, which can only be estimated generally, but never subjected to any regular calculation.
  (b) Because the *emotions* which come into play may make the combat a subject of enthusiasm, and through that a subject for higher judgment.

(41) The combat may therefore be an act of talent and genius, in opposition to calculating reason.

(42) Now the feelings and the genius which manifest themselves in the combat must be regarded as separate moral agencies which, owing to their great diversity and elasticity, incessantly break out beyond the limits of calculating reason.

(43) It is the duty of the Art of War to take account of these forces in theory and in practice.[22]

(44) The more they are used to the utmost, the more vigorous and fruitful of results will be the combat.

(45) All inventions of art, such as arms, organisation, exercise in tactics, the principles of the use of the different arms in the combat, are restrictions on the natural instinct, which has to be led by indirect means to a more efficient use of its powers. But the emotional forces will not submit to be thus clipped, and if we go too far in trying to make instruments of them, we rob them of

[20] The human dimension persists in war and warfare. See *Warfighting*, 13–14.

[21] This is a mental capacity for reason and not the warfighting function, intelligence. No matter how much information we gather about the enemy, how many reports subordinate commanders send up the chain of command, or how many rehearsals, modeling, or simulation are conducted—warfare is always subject to chance.

[22] This is a duty, too, of the military professional. The art of war subsumes the science of war. See *Warfighting*, 18.

their impulse and force. There must, therefore, always be given them a certain room to play between the rules of theory and its practical execution. This entails the necessity of a higher point of view, of great wisdom as respects theory, and great tact of judgment as respects practice.

Two Modes of Fighting—Close Combat and Fire Combat[23]

(46) Of all weapons which have yet been invented by human ingenuity, those which bring the combatants into closest contact, those which are nearest to the pugilistic encounter, are the most natural, and correspond with most instinct. The dagger and the battle-axe are more so than the lance, the javelin, or the sling.[24]

(47) Weapons with which the enemy can be attacked while he is at a distance are more instruments for the understanding; they allow the feelings, the "instinct for fighting" properly called, to remain almost at rest, and this so much the more according as the range of their effects is greater. With a sling we can imagine to ourselves a certain degree of anger accompanying the throw, there is less of this feeling in discharging a musket, and still less in firing a cannon shot.

(48) Although there are shades of difference, still all modern weapons may be placed under one or other of two great classes, that is, the cut-and-thrust weapons, and fire-arms; the former for close combat, the latter for fighting at a distance.

(49) Therefore it follows that there are two modes of fighting— the close combat (hand-to-hand) and the combat with fire-arms.

(50) Both have for their object the destruction of the enemy.

(51) In close combat this effect is quite certain; in the combat with fire-arms it is only more or less probable. From this difference follows a very different signification in the two modes of fighting.

[23] *Close combat* correlates to maneuver, and *fire combat* to firepower or supporting arms.

[24] In the modern context, we are no longer talking about cutting weapons—although the U.S. Marines still employ the Ka-Bar combat knife—but instead the difference between personal and small crew-served weapons and stand-off weapons, like artillery, aircraft, and cyber, electromagnetic, and informational effects.

(52) As the destruction in hand-to-hand fighting is inevitable, the smallest superiority either through advantages or in courage is decisive, and the party at a disadvantage, or inferior in courage, tries to escape the danger by flight.

(53) This occurs so regularly, so commonly, and so soon in all hand-to-hand fights in which several are engaged, that the destructive effects properly belonging to this kind of fight are very much diminished thereby, and its principal effect consists rather in driving the enemy off the field than in destroying him.

(54) If, therefore, we look for the practical effect of close combat, we must place our object not in the *destruction* of the enemy, but in his *expulsion* from the field. The destruction becomes the means.[25]

(55) As in the hand-to-hand fight, originally, the destruction of the enemy was the object, so in the combat with fire-arms the primary object is to put the enemy to flight, and the destruction is only the means. We fire upon the enemy to drive him away, and to spare ourselves the close combat for which we are not prepared.

(56) But the danger caused by the combat with firearms is not quite inevitable, it is only more or less probable: its effect, therefore, is not so great on the senses of individuals, and only becomes great through continuance and through its whole sum, which, as it does not affect the senses so much, is not such a direct impression. It is therefore not essentially necessary that one of the two sides should withdraw from it. From this it follows that one party is not put to flight at once, and in many cases may not be at all.

(57) If this is the case then, as a rule at the conclusion of the combat with fire-arms, the close combat must be resorted to in order to put the enemy to flight.

[25] For more, see the chapter "Ends and Means in War," in Clausewitz, *On War*, vol. 1, book 1, chap. 2, 27–45.

(58) On the other hand, the destructive effect gains in intensity by continuance of the fire combat just as much as it loses in the close combat by the quick decision.

(59) From this it follows that instead of the putting the enemy to flight being the general object of the fire combat, that object is to be looked for in the direct effect of the applied means, that is, in the destruction and weakening of the enemy's forces.

(60) If the object of the close combat is to *drive the enemy from the field*, that of the combat with fire-arms to *destroy his armed force*, then the former is the real instrument for the *decisive stroke*, the latter is to be regarded as *the preparation*.[26]

(61) In each, however, there is a certain amount of the effect pertaining to both principles. The close combat is not devoid of destructive efforts, neither is the combat with fire-arms ineffectual to drive the enemy off the field.

(62) The destructive effect of the close combat is in most cases extremely insignificant, very often it amounts to nil; it would, therefore, hardly be taken account of if it did not sometimes become of considerable importance by increasing the number of prisoners.

(63) But it is well to observe that these cases generally occur after the fire has produced considerable effect.

(64) Close combat in the existing relation of arms would, therefore, have but an insignificant destructive effect without the assistance of fire.

(65) The destructive force of fire-arms in combat may by continuance be intensified to the utmost extremity, that is, to the shaking and extinction of courage.

[26] Fire combat enables victory; only maneuver delivers it.

(66) The consequence of that is, that by far the greatest share in the destruction of the enemy's combatant powers is due to the effect of fire-arms.

(67) The weakening of the enemy through the fire combat either—
    (a) Causes his retreat, or
    (b) Serves as a preparation for the hand-to-hand encounter.

(68) By putting the enemy to flight, which is the object of the hand-to-hand combat, the real victory may be attained, because driving the enemy from the field constitutes a victory. If the whole mass engaged is small, then such a victory may embrace the whole, and be a decisive result.[27]

(69) But when the close combat has only taken place between portions of the whole mass of forces, or when several close combats in succession make up the whole combat, then the result in a single one can only be considered as a victory in a *partial combat.*

(70) If the conquered division is a considerable part of the whole, then in its defeat it may carry the whole along with it; and, thus, from the victory over a part, a victory over the whole may immediately follow.

(71) Even if a success in close combat does not amount to a victory over the mass of the enemy's forces, still it always ensures the following advantages:
    (a) Gain of ground.
    (b) Shaking of moral force.
    (c) Disorder in the enemy's ranks.
    (d) Destruction of physical force.

(72) In a partial combat, the fire combat is therefore to be regarded as a destroying act, the close combat as a decisive act. How these points are to be reviewed in relation to the total combat we shall consider at a future time.

[27] It is worth pausing to consider the degree to which, today, merely driving the enemy from the battlefield, even if we consider an expanded battlespace, is sufficient for victory. While driving the enemy from the battlefield may be the precursor to success, Clausewitz emphasizes the need to capitalize on those gains, often through the use of reserves, to reinforce success or to conduct a pursuit and then a rout. See Clausewitz, *On War*, vol. 1, book 4, chap. 13, 305–7. This is true at a tactical level of individual battles and at a strategic level for campaigns. See Clausewitz's military history of Waterloo and the Campaign of 1815: Carl von Clausewitz, *On Waterloo: Clausewitz, Wellington, and the Campaign of 1815*, ed. and trans. Christopher Bassford, Daniel Moran, and Gregory W. Pedlow (CreateSpace, 2015). The point is that what matters for the victory—however it is defined by the character of warfare at the time—is how it is used, as strategy, to achieve political ends.

Relation of the two Forms of Combat in regard to Attack and Defence[28]

(73) The combat consists, further, of attack and defence.

(74) The attack is the *positive* intention, the defence the *negative*. The first aims at *putting* the enemy *to flight*; the latter merely at *keeping possession*.

(75) But this *keeping possession* is no mere *holding out*, not passive endurance; its success depends on a vigorous reaction. This reaction is the destruction of the attacking forces. Therefore, it is only the *object*, not the *means*, which is to be regarded as *negative*.

(76) But as it follows of itself that if the defender maintains his position the adversary must give way, therefore, although the defender has the negative object, the retreat, that is, the giving way of the enemy, is the sign of victory also for the defender.

(77) Naturally, on account of a like object, the close combat is the element of attack.

(78) But as close combat contains in itself so little of the destructive principle, the assailant who confines himself to the use of it alone would hardly be considered as a combatant in most cases, and in any case would play a very unequal game.

(79) Except when small bodies only are engaged, or bodies consisting entirely of cavalry, the close combat can never constitute the whole attack. The larger the masses engaged, the more artillery and infantry come into play, the less will it suffice for the end.

(80) The attack must, therefore, also include in itself as much of the fire combat as is necessary.

(81) In this, that is, in the fire combat, both sides are to be regarded as upon an equality, so far as respects the mode of fighting.

[28] This section presages similar concepts in *On War*, by which point the concept has become offense and defense. The concept retains focus on positive and negative aims, however. Defense may be the stronger form of warfare, but it can only preserve gains. Only the offense can increase them.

Therefore, the greater the proportion of fighting with fire-arms as compared with close combat, the more the original inequality between attack and defence is diminished. As regards the remaining disadvantages of the close combat, to which the assailant must ultimately have recourse, they must be compensated for by such advantages as are inherent in that form, and by superiority of numbers.

(82) The fire combat is the natural element of the defensive.

(83) When a successful result (the retreat of the assailant) is obtained by that form of combat, there is no necessity to have recourse to close combat.

(84) When that result is not obtained, and the assailant resorts to close combat, the defender must do the same.

(85) Generally, the defence does not by any means exclude the close combat, if the advantages to be expected from it appear greater than those of the combat with fire-arms.

Advantageous Conditions in both Forms of Combat

(86) We must now examine more closely the nature in general of both combats, in order to ascertain the points which give the preponderance in the same.

(87) *The fire combat.*
- (a) Superiority in the use of arms (this depends on the organisation and the quality of the troops).
- (b) Superiority in the formation (tactical organisation) and the elementary tactics as established dispositions. ... In a question of the employment of regularly disciplined troops in the combat, these things do not come into consideration, because they are supposed to belong to the idea of troops. But, as a subject of the theory of the combat in its *widest sense*, they may and should be considered.

Notes

(c) The number.
(d) The form of the line of battle so far as it is not already contained in *b*.
(e) The ground.

(88) As we are only now treating of *the employment of disciplined troops*, we have nothing to do with *a* and *b*, they are only to be taken into consideration as given quantities.

(89a) *Superiority of numbers.*[29]
If two unequal bodies of infantry or artillery are drawn up opposite to each other on parallel lines of the same extent, then if every shot fired is directed like a *target shot* against a separate individual, the number of hits will be in proportion to the number of men firing. The proportion of hits would bear just the same relation if the shots were directed against a full target—therefore if the mark was no longer a single man, but a battalion, a line, &c. This is, indeed, also the way in which the *shots* fired by skirmishers in War may for the most part be estimated. But here the target is not full; instead of that it is a line of men with intervals between them. The intervals *decrease* as the number of men increases in a given space; consequently, the effect of a fire combat between bodies of troops of unequal number will be a sum made out of the number of those firing, and the number of the enemy's troops they are firing against; that is, in other words, the superiority in number in a fire combat produces no preponderating effect, because that which is gained through the number of shots is lost again through a greater number of the enemy's taking effect.

Suppose that 50 men place themselves upon the same extent of ground as 500 opposite to them. Let 30 shots out of 50 be supposed to strike the target, that is, the quadrilateral occupied by the enemy's battalion; then, out of the enemy's 500 shots 300 will strike the quadrilateral occupied by our fifty men. But the 500 men stand ten times as close as the 50, therefore our balls hit ten times as many as the enemy's, and thus, by our 50 shots, exactly as many of the enemy are hit as are hit on our side by his 500.[30]

[29] In *Fleet Tactics*, Capt Wayne P. Hughes Jr. describes the importance of Lanchester Equations to naval combat. This is extended to salvo models for modern missile combat. Hughes, *Fleet Tactics and Naval Operations*, 3d ed. (Annapolis, MD: Naval Institute Press, 2018), 30, 263.

[30] While the specifics of this mathematical interlude are somewhat out of character for the rest of his work, Clausewitz's use of hypothetical thought experiments is not. These "if, then" formulations are more common in his historical analyses. A similar mathematical interlude is found in book 3, chapter 12. Both are worth puzzling through.

Although this result does not exactly correspond with the reality, and there is a small advantage in general on the side of the superior numbers, still there is no doubt that it is essentially correct; and that the efficacy on either side, that is, the result in a combat with fire-arms, far from keeping exact pace with the superiority in numbers, is scarcely increased at all by that superiority.

This result is of the utmost importance, for it constitutes the basis of that economy of forces in the preparatory destructive act which may be regarded as one of the surest means to victory.

(89b) Let it not be thought that this result may lead to an absurdity; and that, for example, two men (the smallest number who can take up the line of our supposed target) must do just as much execution as 2,000, provided that the two men are placed at a distance apart equal to the front of the 2,000. If the 2,000 always fired directly to their front, that might be the case. But if the number of the weaker side is so small that the stronger directs his concentrated fire upon individuals, then naturally there must follow a great difference in the effect, for, in such a case, our supposition of simple target-firing is set aside. Likewise, a very weak line of fire would never oblige the enemy to engage in a fire-combat: instead of that, such a line would be driven from the field by him at once. We see, therefore, that the foregoing result is not to be carried to an extreme in application, but yet it is of great importance for the reasons given. Hundreds of times a line of fire has maintained its own against one of twice its strength, and it is easy to see what consequences may result from that in the economy of force.[31]

(89c) We may, therefore, say that either of the opposing sides has it in his power to increase or reduce the mutual, that is, the total effect of the fire, according as he brings or does not bring more combatants into the line which is firing.

(90) *The form of the line of battle may be:*
   (a) With parallel fronts of equal length; then it is the same for both sides.

.

[31] Economy of force demands that we must not *fail* to make effective use of all the assets available. See *Tactics*, MCDP 1-3 (Washington, DC: Headquarters Marine Corps, 1997), 33.

   (b) With parallel front, but outflanking the enemy; then it is advantageous (but, as we may easily conceive, the advantage is small, on account of the limited range of fire-arms).

   (c) Enveloping. This is advantageous on account of the double effect of the shots, and because the greater extent of front follows of itself from that form.

Forms the reverse of *b* and *c* are obviously disadvantageous.

(91) *Ground* is advantageous in combat with fire-arms—

   (a) By affording cover like a breastwork.

   (b) By intercepting the view of the enemy, thus forming an obstacle to his taking aim.

   (c) As an obstacle to approach, by which the enemy is kept long under our fire, and impeded in the delivery of his own fire.

(92) In close combat the advantages afforded by ground are the same as in fire combat.

(93) The two first subjects (*a* and *b* No. 87) do not come into consideration here. But we must observe that superiority in the use of weapons does not make as great a difference in close combat as in the fire combat; and, on the other hand, courage plays a most decisive part. The subjects touched upon under *b* (No. 87) are especially important for cavalry, the arm by which most close combats are fought.[32]

(94) In close combat *number* is much more decisive than in the combat with fire-arms, it is almost the chief thing.

(95) *The form of the order of battle* is also much more decisive than in the combat with fire-arms, and when the front is parallel, a small instead of a great extent of front is the most advantageous.

[32] (87) *The fire combat.*
    (a) Superiority in the use of arms (this depends on the organisation and the quality of
       the troops).
    (b) Superiority in the formation (tactical organisation) and the elementary tactics as es-
       tablished dispositions.
As found on p. 54.

(96) *The ground—*
    (a) As obstacle to approach. In this consists by far its greatest efficacy in close combat.
    (b) As a means of concealment. This favours a surprise, which is especially important in close combat.

Analysis of the Combat

(97) In No. 23 we have seen that every combat is a whole, composed of many members or parts, in which the independence of the parts is very unequal, inasmuch as it diminishes by a descending scale. We shall now examine this point more closely.[33]

(98) We can easily imagine as a *single member*, such a number as can be led into the fight by the *word of command*; for instance, a Battalion, a Battery, or a Regiment of cavalry, if these masses are really in close order.

(99) When the Word of Command no longer suffices, a written or verbal Order commences.

(100) The Word of Command admits of no gradations, in point of fact it is a part of the execution. But the Order has degrees, from the utmost distinctness, approaching to the Word of Command, down to the utmost generality. It is not the execution itself, but only a commission to execute.

(101) No one subject to the Word of Command has any will of his own; but, whenever instead of that Word an Order is given, a certain independence of members begins because the Order is of a general nature, and the will of the Leader must supply any insufficiency in its terms.[34]

(102) If a combat admitted of being perfectly prearranged and foreseen in all its coincident and successive parts and events, if, that is to say, its plan could descend into the minutest details, as in the construction of a piece of inanimate machinery, then the Order would have none of this indefiniteness.

[33] (23) In reality, every combat may be separated into as many single combats as there are combatants. But the individual only appears as a separate item when he fights singly, that is, independently. As found on p. 38.

[34] Here, we can start to find the seeds of mission command, in particular commander's intent.

(103) But belligerents do not cease to be men, and individuals can never be converted into machines having no will of their own; and the ground on which they fight will seldom or never be a complete and bare level, which can exercise no influence on the combat. It is, therefore, quite impossible to calculate beforehand all that is to take place.[35]

(104) This insufficiency of plan increases with the duration of the combat, and with the number of the combatants. The close combat of a small troop is almost completely contained in its plan; but the plan for a combat with fire-arms of even very small bodies can never be thoroughly complete to the same degree, on account of its duration and the incidents which spring up. Then again, the close combat of large masses, as, for instance, of a Cavalry Division of 2,000 or 3,000 horse, cannot be carried out so completely in conformity with the original plan that the will of its single leaders is not frequently obliged to supply something. As for the plan for a great battle, except as regards the preliminary part, it can only be a very general outline.

(105) As this insufficiency of plan (disposition) increases with the time and space which the combat takes, so, therefore, as a rule, a greater margin for contingencies must be allowed to large than to smaller bodies of troops, and the Order will increase in its precision as it descends the scale down to those parts which are governed by Word of Command.

(106) Further, the independence of the parts will also differ according to the circumstances in which they are placed. Space, time, the character of the ground and country, and nature of the duty will diminish or increase this independence as respects one and the same subdivision.

(107) Besides this systematic division of the entire combat into separate parts according to plan, a casual division may also take place thus:

[35] This is the beginning of mission-type orders.

    (a) By our views expanding beyond the limits of the original plan.

    (b) By an unforeseen separation of parts, which we intended to have kept under Word of Command.

(108) This fresh division depends on circumstances which cannot be foreseen.

(109) The consequence is unequal result in parts which should have been all united as one whole (because, in point of fact, they become placed in different relations).

(110) Thus arises, at certain parts, the necessity for a change not contemplated in the general plan,

    (a) That these parts may avoid disadvantages of ground, or of numbers, or of position.

    (b) That advantages gained in all these different respects may be turned to account.

(111) The consequence of this is that, involuntarily, often more or less designedly, a fire combat passes into close combat, or the other way, the latter into the former.

(112) The problem, then, is to make these changes fit into the general plan, so that—

    (a) If they lead to a disadvantage, it may be remedied in one way or another.

    (b) If they lead to a success it may be used as far as possible, short of exposing us to the risk of a reverse.

(113) It is, therefore, the intentional or unintentional division of the total combat into a greater or less number of minor, independent combats, which causes the form of combat to change from close combat to fire combat, as well as from attack to defence, during the total combat.

Now the whole still remains to be considered in this relation.

Notes

The Combat consists of two Acts— the Destructive and the Decisive Act[36]

(114) From the fire combat, with its destructive principle, and from the close combat with its principle of putting to flight, according to No. 72, proceed two different acts in the partial combat, the destructive and the decisive act.[37]

(115) The smaller the masses are, the more these two acts will resolve themselves into one simple fire combat, or one close combat.

(116) The greater the masses the more must these two acts be taken in a collective sense, in such manner that the destructive act is made up of a number of simultaneous and successive fire combats; and the decisive act in the same manner, of several close combats.

(117) In this manner the division of the combat not only continues, but also extends itself more and more, the greater the masses brought into conflict; whilst the destructive act and the decisive act are further and further separated from each other in time.

The Destructive Act

(118) The greater the mass of troops, the more important becomes the physical destruction, for—

- (a) The influence of the Commander is so much the less. (His influence is greater in close combat than in fire combat.)
- (b) The moral inequality is so much less. With large masses, whole Armies for instance, there is nothing but the difference of nationality; whilst in smaller bodies there is to be added that of corps and of individuals; and, lastly, of special accidental circumstances, which in large bodies *balance* each other.
- (c) The order of battle is so much the deeper, that is, there are so many more reserves to renew the combat, as we shall see in the sequel. The number of partial combats, therefore, increases, and consequently the duration of

[36] This section is a logical extension of the previous section on fire combat and close combat. Fire combat provides combat with the destructive act. Close combat provides it with the decisive act. Both must work in harmony to achieve victory.

[37] (72) In a partial combat, the fire combat is therefore to be regarded as a destroying act, the close combat as a decisive act. As found on p. 50.

the total combat, and by that means the influence of the first moment, which is so very decisive in putting the enemy to flight, is lessened.

(119) From the preceding number it follows that the greater the mass of the Army, the greater must be the physical destruction as a preparation for the decision.

(120) This preparation consists in this, that the number of combatants diminishes on both sides, but the relation alters in our favour.

(121) The first of these is sufficient, if we are already morally or physically superior; the second is requisite, if such is not the case.

(122) The destruction of the enemy's combatant force is made up—
 (a) Of all that are put physically *hors de combat*—killed, wounded, and prisoners.[38]
 (b) Of whatever part is spent physically and morally.

(123) After a fire combat of several hours' duration, in which a body of troops has suffered severe loss, for instance, a quarter or one-third of its numbers, the *débris* may, for the time, be looked upon as a heap of burnt-out cinders, for—[39]
 (a) The men are physically exhausted.
 (b) They have spent their ammunition.
 (c) Their arms want cleaning.
 (d) Many have left the field with the wounded, although not themselves wounded.
 (e) The rest think they have done their part for the day, and if once they get beyond the sphere of danger do not willingly return to it.
 (f) The feeling of courage with which they started has had the edge taken off, the longing for the fight is satisfied.
 (g) The original organisation and formation are partly destroyed, or thrown into disorder.

[38] *Hors de combat* is French for "out of combat" and refers to those who are incapable of acting in war.

[39] The mental and moral effects of being exposed to sustained fires.

(124) The consequences, *e* and *f*, make their appearance, more or less, according as the combat has been successful or the reverse. A body of troops which has gained ground, or successfully maintained the original position assigned to it, can be made further use of more easily than one that has been repulsed.

(125a) There are two deductions from No. 123 which we must bring under notice.

The first is the *economy of force*, which is made by the use of a smaller number of men in the combat with fire-arms than the enemy employs. For, if the dilapidation of forces in the fire combat consists not only in the loss of those placed *hors de combat*, but further in this, that all who have fought are lowered in their powers; then, naturally, this lowering of powers will be less on that side which brings the fewest troops into action.

If 500 men have been able to maintain their ground against 1000, if the losses are equal on each side, say 200 men, then on the one side there will remain 800 men who are fatigued, while the other side will have 800, of whom 300 are fatigued, but 500 are fresh.

(125b) The second deduction is that the weakening of the enemy, consequently the *dilapidation of the enemy's combative power*, is of much greater extent than the mere number of killed, wounded, and prisoners would seem to represent. This number amounts to, perhaps, only one-sixth of the whole; there should, therefore, remain five-sixths. But out of that five-sixths, in all probability only the *untouched reserve*, and some troops, which, although they have been in action, have suffered very little, are, in reality, to be regarded as serviceable, and the remainder (perhaps four-sixths) may be looked upon for the present as a *caput mortuum*.[40]

(126) This diminution of the efficient mass is the first aim of the destructive act; the real decision can only be accomplished by smaller masses of troops.

[40] *Caput mortuum* is Latin for "dead head" or "worthless remains." The term comes from alchemy and refers to the remains of an alchemical process after which the result is unchangeable.

(127) But—although the absolute size of the masses is not an un-important matter, as fifty men opposed to fifty can proceed to a decision on the spot, while 50,000 opposed to 50,000 cannot do so—still it is the relative, *not the absolute* size of the masses, which is an obstacle to the decision. Thus if five-sixths of the whole have measured their powers in the destructive act, then both Generals, even if they have continued on an equality, will be much nearer to the final resolution which they have to make, and it is only a relatively small impulse which is required to bring on the decisive act. It is all the same whether the sixth part remaining is a sixth of an Army of 30,000, therefore 5,000 men, or one-sixth of an Army of 150,000 men, that is, 25,000 men.

(128) The principal object of each side in the destructive act is to work out for itself a preponderance for the decisive act.

(129) This superiority can be obtained by the destruction of the enemy's physical force, but it may also be obtained by the other causes enumerated under No. 4.[41]

(130) There is, therefore, in the destructive act a natural endeavour to profit by all the advantages which offer as far as circumstances will admit.

(131) Now the combat of large masses is always split into several partial combats (No. 23) which are more or less independent, and therefore must frequently contain in themselves both a destructive and a decisive act, if the advantages obtained from the first of these acts are to be turned to account.[42]

(132) Through the skilful and successful mixture of the close combat, we chiefly obtain the advantages which are to be derived from shaking the enemy's courage, creating disorder in his ranks, and gaining ground.

[41] (4) The enemy is moved to [evacuate the battlefield]:
    (a) If his loss is excessive,
        (i) . . . fears he will be overpowered,
        (ii) . . . the object will cost him too much.
    (b) . . . formation of his Army . . . is too much shaken.
    (c) . . . fear excessive loss if he continues the combat.
    (d) . . . order of battle is attended with too great disadvantages.
    (e) . . . taken by surprise . . . or suddenly attacked.
    (f) . . . perceives that his opponent is too superior.
    (g) . . . opponent has too great a superiority in moral forces.
As found on p. 30.

[42] (23) In reality, every combat may be separated into as many single combats as there are combatants. But the individual only appears as a separate item when he fights singly, that is, independently. As found on p. 38.

(133) Even the physical destruction of the enemy's forces is very much increased by that means, for prisoners can only be made in close combat.

Thus we may conceive that if an enemy's Battalion is shaken by our fire, if our bayonet attack drives it out of an advantageous position, and we follow him in his flight with a couple of Squadrons, this partial success may place important advantages of all kinds in the scale of the general result; but then it is a condition that it be done without involving this victorious troop in difficulty, for if our Battalion and our Squadron through this means should fall into the hands of superior forces of the enemy, then this partial decision has been ill-timed.[43]

(134) The utilising of these partial successes is in the hands of the subordinate Commanders, and gives a great advantage to an Army which has experienced officers at the head of its Divisions, Brigades, Regiments, Battalions, Batteries, &c.

(135) Thus each of the two Commanders seeks to obtain for himself in the course of the destructive act those advantages which bring about the decision, and at all events pave the way for it.

(136) The most important of these objects are always captured guns and ground gained.

(137) The importance of the latter is increased if the enemy has made it an object to defend a strong position.

(138) Thus the destructive act on both sides, but especially on that of the assailant, is a cautious advance towards the object.

(139) As numbers are so little decisive in the fire combat (No. 53), therefore the endeavour naturally follows to keep up the combat with as few troops as possible.[44]

[43] *Squadrons* here refers to horse cavalry which, at the time, were organized in squadrons.

.

[44] (53) This occurs so regularly, so commonly, and so soon in all hand-to-hand fights in which several are engaged, that the destructive effects properly belonging to this kind of fight are very much diminished thereby, and its principal effect consists rather in driving the enemy off the field than in destroying him. As found on p. 46.

(140) As the fire combat predominates in the destructive act, therefore the greatest economy of force must be the prevailing principle in the same.

(141) As numerical force is so essential in close combat, therefore for the decision of partial combats in the destructive act, superior numbers must frequently be employed.

(142) But upon the whole the character of thrift must rule here also, and, in general, only those decisions are to the purpose which realise themselves of themselves as it were, without any great preponderance of numbers.

(143) An inopportune endeavour to gain the decision leads to the following consequences:
   (a) If it is undertaken with economy of our forces, we get involved with superior forces.
   (b) If the requisite force is used, we get exhausted before the right time.

(144) The question whether it is opportune to try for a decision recurs very frequently during the destructive act, nevertheless, as respects the great ultimate decision, it presents itself at the end of the destructive act.

(145) The destructive act on this account naturally strives at certain points to pass into the decisive act, because no advantage developed in the course of that act will attain completeness except through the decisive act, which is its necessary complement.

(146) The more fruitful in results the means applied in the destructive act are, or the greater the physical and moral superiority, the stronger will be this tendency of the whole.

(147) But when the results are small or negative, or when the enemy has the superiority, this tendency likewise may be so rare

Notes

and so feeble at isolated points that, as respects the whole, it is much the same as if it did not exist at all.

(148) This natural tendency may lead to ill-timed decisions in partial combats as well as in the total combat, but it is very far from being an evil on that account; it is rather a necessary property of the destructive act, because without it much would be neglected.

(149) The judgment of the Leader at each point, and of the Commander-in-Chief in the total combat, must determine whether an opportunity which presents itself is advantageous for a decisive blow or not, that is, whether it may not lead to a counter blow, and thus to a *negative* result.[45]

(150) The conduct of a combat in relation to the preparation preceding the decisive stroke, or rather the preparation expressly for that stroke, consists, therefore, in organising a fire combat, and, in a wider sense, a destructive act, and giving to it a proportionate duration, that is, in only proceeding to the decisive stroke when it appears that the destructive act has produced sufficient effect.

(151) The judgment on this point must be guided less by the clock, that is, less by the mere relations of time, than by the events which have taken place, by the evident signs of a superiority having been obtained.

(152) Now as the destructive act, if attended with good results, strives already of itself towards the decisive act, therefore the duty of the Chief consists principally in determining when and where the moment arrives to give the reins to this tendency.

(153) If the tendency towards the decisive act is very weak during the destructive act, that is a tolerably sure sign that victory cannot be calculated on.

(154) In such a case, therefore, the Chief and his Generals will usually not give but receive the decisive shock.

[45] It is important to note that by *Commander-in-Chief* Clausewitz means the overall commander of the unit and not the president nor any other political leadership.

(155) If still it must be given, then it takes place by an express order, which must be accompanied by the use of all the personal means of inspiriting the men, all the stimulating influence which the General has at his command.

The Decisive Act

(156) The decision is that event which produces in one of the Generals a resolution to quit the field.[46]

(157) The grounds for quitting the field we have given in No. 4. These grounds may come forth gradually by one small disaster after another being heaped up in the course of the destructive act, and the resolution may, therefore, be taken without a really decisive event. In such a case no decisive act in particular takes place.[47]

(158) But the resolution may also be produced by one single, very disastrous event, therefore, suddenly, when up to that moment everything has been evenly balanced.

(159) Then that act of the enemy which has called forth this resolution is to be regarded as the decisive act.

(160) The most common case is that the decision ripens gradually in the course of the destructive act, but the resolution of the vanquished gets its final impulse from some particular event. Therefore, in this case also, the decisive act is to be considered as having been given.

(161) If a decisive act is given, then it must be a positive action—
    (a) It may be an attack; or
    (b) It may be only the advance of reserves hitherto held under cover.

(162) With small bodies, close combat by a single charge is often decisive.

[46] Defeat is a decision in the mind of one or the other commander.

[47] (4) The enemy is moved to [evacuate the battlefield]:
    (a) If his loss is excessive,
        (i) . . . fears he will be overpowered,
        (ii) . . . the object will cost him too much.
    (b) . . . formation of his Army . . . is too much shaken.
    (c) . . . fear excessive loss if he continues the combat.
    (d) . . . order of battle is attended with too great disadvantages.
    (e) . . . taken by surprise . . . or suddenly attacked.
    (f) . . . perceives that his opponent is too superior.
    (g) . . . opponent has too great a superiority in moral forces.
As found on p. 30.

(163) When larger masses are engaged, the attack by means of close combat may also suffice, but a single charge will then hardly be sufficient.

(164) If the masses are still larger, there is then a mixture of the fire combat, as in the case of horse artillery supporting the charge of heavy masses of cavalry.

(165) With great bodies composed of all arms, a decision can never result from close combat alone, a renewed fire combat is necessary.

(166) But this renewed fire combat will be of the nature of an attack itself, it will be carried out in close masses, therefore with an action concentrated in time and space, as a short preparation for the real attack.

(167) When the decision is not the result of a particular close combat, but of a number of simultaneous and consecutive combats of both kinds, it then becomes a distinct act belonging to the entire combat, as has been already said in a general way (No. 115).[48]

(168) In this act the close combat predominates.

(169) In the same measure as the close combat predominates, so will also the offensive, although at certain points the defensive may be preserved.

(170) Towards the close of a battle the line of retreat is always regarded with increased jealousy, therefore a threat against that line is always then a potent means of bringing on the decision.

(171) On that account, when circumstances permit, the plan of the battle will be aimed at that point from the very first.

[48] (115) The smaller the masses are, the more these two acts will resolve themselves into one simple fire combat, or one close combat. As found on p. 68.

(172) The more the battle, or combat, develops itself in the sense of a plan of this kind, so much the more seriously the enemy's line of retreat will be menaced.

(173) Another great step towards victory is breaking the order of formation.[49] The regular formation in which the troops commence the action suffers considerably in the long destructive combats, in which they themselves wring out their strength. If this wear and tear and exhaustion has reached a certain point, then a rapid advance in concentrated masses on one side against the line of battle of the other may produce a degree of disorder which forbids the latter any longer to think of victory, and calls in requisition all his powers to place the separate parts of his line in safety, and to restore the connection of the whole in the best way he can for the moment.

(174) From what precedes it is evident that, as in the preparatory acts, the utmost economy of force must predominate, so in the decisive act, to win the mastery through numbers must be the ruling idea.

(175) Just as in the preparatory acts, endurance, firmness, and coolness are the first qualities, so in the decisive act, boldness and fiery spirit must predominate.

(176) Usually only one of the opposing Commanders delivers the deciding stroke, the other receives it.

(177) As long as all continues in equilibrium, he who gives the decisive blow may be—
    (a) The assailant; or
    (b) The defender.

(178) As the assailant has the positive object, it is most natural that he should deliver it; and, therefore, this is what occurs most frequently.

[49] Today, this is referred to as *disruption* or *disintegration*. Disruption occurs when a military force is disordered or delayed by enemy action. Disintegration occurs when a military force cannot fight as a united whole. For example, if an infantry battalion loses communication with its companies and its supporting arms, it no longer functions as a battalion, but rather a group of uncoordinated, lesser units.

(179) But if the equilibrium is much disturbed, then the decision may be given—
    (a) By the Commander who has the advantage.
    (b) By the one who is under the disadvantage.

(180) The first is plainly more natural; and if this Commander is also the assailant, it is still more natural: therefore, there are few cases in which the decision does not emanate from him.

(181) But if the defender is the party who has the advantage, then it is also natural that he should give the decision, so that the relative situation which is produced by degrees has more influence than the original intention of offensive and defensive.[50]

(182) When the decision is given by the assailant, although he has palpably the disadvantage, it looks like a last attempt to gain his original object. If the defender, who has gained advantages, gives him time to do so, it is certainly consistent with the nature of the positive intention of the assailant to make such a last attempt.

(183a) A defender who, although decidedly at a disadvantage, still proceeds to give the decision, does that which is contrary to the nature of things, and which may be regarded as an act of desperation.

(183b) The result in the decisive stage is conformable to the relations just developed; so that, as a rule, it will only be favourable to the side which gives the decision if he is naturally led to do so by the relations in which he stands.

(184) When all is still in a state of equilibrium the result is generally favourable to the side which gives the decision, for at the moment when a battle is ripe for decision, when the forces have worn themselves out on each other, the positive principle is of much greater weight than at the commencement.

[50] Initiative is usually, but not always, associated with the offense. Here, Clausewitz discusses how either side can obtain it. See *Warfighting*, 32–35.

(185) The General who receives the decision may either determine on an immediate retreat in consequence, and decline all further combat, or he may continue the combat.

(186) If he continues the engagement he can only do so as—
   (a) A commencement of his retreat, because he wants time to make the requisite arrangements; or
   (b) A virtual struggle through which he still hopes for victory.

(187) If the General who *accepts* the decision stands in very favourable relations, he may in so doing also adhere to the defensive.

(188a) But if the decision proceeds naturally from the advantageous situation of the side giving it, then the General who accepts it must also pass over to a more or less active defence, that is, he must oppose attack by attack, partly because the natural advantages of the defence (*position, order, surprise*) wear themselves out by degrees in the course of the combat, and, at last, there is not enough of them left; partly because (as we have said in No. 184) the positive principle acquires incessantly more and more weight.

Their Separation as regards Time
(188b) The view here propounded, that every combat is composed of two separate acts, will meet with strong opposition at first sight.

(189) This opposition will proceed partly from a false view of the combat, which has become habitual, partly from an over-pedantic importance being ascribed to the idea of such a division.

(190) We imagine to ourselves the opposition between attack and defence as too decided, the two activities as too completely antithetical, or, rather, we assume the antithesis to be where it is not to be found in practice.

Notes

(191) From this it results that we imagine the assailant, from the first moment to the last, as steadily and unremittingly striving to advance, and every modification in that advance as an entirely involuntary and compulsory one, which proceeds *directly* from the resistance encountered.

(192) According to this idea nothing would be more natural than that every attack should begin with the energy of an assault.

(193) Still even those who adhere to this kind of idea have become accustomed to a preparatory act on the part of the artillery, because it was too plain that without it an assault would generally be useless.

(194) But otherwise that absolute tendency to advance to the attack has been considered so natural that an attack without a shot being fired is looked upon as the ideal of perfection. Even Frederick the Great, up to the time of the battle of Zorndorf, looked upon fire in the attack as something exceptional.[51]

(195) Although there has since been a disposition to modify that notion, still there are numbers at the present time who think that the assailant *cannot* make himself master of the important points in a position *too soon.*

(196) Those who make the greatest concessions to fire, at the same time advocate an immediate advance to the attack, the delivery of a few volleys by Battalions close to the enemy's position, and then an onset with the bayonet.

(197) But military history and a glance at the nature of our arms show that absolutely to despise the use of fire in the attack is an absurdity.[52]

(198) A little acquaintance with the nature of the combat and, above all, actual experience, teach us also that a body of troops which has been engaged under fire is seldom fit for a vigorous

[51] The Battle of Zorndorf occurred in 1758 between Prussian forces under Frederick the Great and Russian forces under William Fermor, during the Seven Years' War (also known as the Third Silesian War). The battle was inconclusive and featured repeated, bloody assaults by Prussian infantry against Russian defensive positions. Clausewitz is perhaps alluding to Frederick learning not to resort to unprepared, frontal attacks because of this battle.

[52] Attacks that are not first enabled by supporting arms are foolish.

assault. Therefore, the concession mentioned in No. 196 is worth nothing.

(199) Lastly, military history gives instances without number in which, owing to a premature advance, advantages previously gained have had to be abandoned with serious loss. Therefore, the principle mentioned in No. 195 is also not admissible.

(200) We maintain accordingly, that the idea now alluded to of an unmixed kind of attack, if we may use the expression, is entirely false, because it only answers to a very few extremely exceptional cases.[53]

(201) But if a commencement with close combat and a decision without preparation in a great battle are not consistent with the nature of things, then of itself there arises a distinction between the *preparation by fire* for the decision and the *decision itself,* therefore, between the two acts which we have been discussing.

(202) We have granted that this distinction may fall to the ground in affairs which are quite of a minor nature (as, for instance, between small bodies of cavalry). The question now is whether it does not also come to an end if the masses attain to certain proportions; not as to whether the employment of fire might cease, for that would be a contradiction in itself, but whether the sharp distinction between the two activities ceases, so that they can no longer be considered as two separate acts.

(203) It may perhaps be maintained that a Battalion should fire before it charges with the bayonet; the one must precede the other, and thus two different acts take place, but only as regards the Battalion, not as respects the greater subdivision of the Brigade, &c. These have no fire period and decision period; they seek to come in contact with the object pointed out to them as speedily as possible, and must leave the way in which it is to be done to the Battalions.

[53] This idea has survived until modern times with an addition. One current planning conception is the division of tactical plans into a shaping phase, a decisive phase, and a sustaining phase. Here, Clausewitz is talking about the first two: *preparation by fire* is the shaping phase and *decision itself* is the decisive phase. See *Marine Corps Operations*, MCDP 1-0 w/change 1 (Washington, DC: Headquarters Marine Corps, 2017), 2-31 and 2-32, for the concepts of an enabling force, decisive force, exploitation force, and sustaining force.

(204) Do we not perceive that in this way all unity would be lost? As one Battalion fights quite close to another, the successes and reverses of one must have a necessary influence on others, and as the effect of our musketry fire is so small that it requires considerable duration to make it efficacious, the influence just noticed must be greater and more decisive through that duration. Even on this ground alone there must be, for the Brigade as well as for the Battalion, a certain general division of time as respects the destructive and the decisive combats.

(205) But another more substantial reason is, that for the decision we are glad to use fresh troops, at least troops that have not been engaged in the destructive act; but these must be taken from the reserve, and the reserves, by their nature, are common property, and on that account cannot be divided beforehand amongst the Battalions.

(206) Now, as the necessity of a division in the combat passes on from the Battalion to the Brigade, therefore from that it passes on to the Division, and from the Division to still larger bodies.

(207) But as the parts of a whole (divisions of the first order) always become more independent the larger the whole is, therefore it is true the unity of the whole will also press less stringently on them, and thus it happens that in the course of a partial combat more decisive acts may and will always take place according as the whole is greater.

(208) The decisions, when Corps are large, will therefore not unite themselves into a whole to the same degree as in the case of Corps of smaller size, but will distribute themselves more as regards time and space; still, between the beginning and the end, a notable distinction between the two different acts is always observable.[54]

(209) Now the parts may be so large, and their separation from each other so wide, that although their action in the combat is

54 Clausewitz considers a corps between 30,000 and 40,000 troops to be of a "consider-able size." Clausewitz, *On War*, vol. 2, book 5, chap. 5, 30.

certainly still directed by the will of one General (a necessary condition to constitute an independent combat), yet this direction limits itself to instructions at the commencement, or at most to a few orders in the course of the combat; in this case, such a part has in itself almost complete power to organise its whole combat.[55]

(210) The more important the decisions which rest with a Corps by its situation, so much the more they will influence the decision of the whole; indeed, we may even suppose the relation of some parts to be such that in their decisions that of the whole is at once contained, and, therefore, a separate decisive act for the whole is no longer required.

(211) *Example*—In a great battle, in which the parts of the Army of the first rank are Corps, a Brigade may receive the order at the commencement to take a village. For this purpose it will make use for itself of its destructive act and its decisive act. Now, the taking of this village may have, more or less, an influence on the ultimate decision of the whole; but it is not in the nature of things that it should greatly influence, and much less that it should effect, that decision of itself, because a Brigade is too small a body to give a decision at the commencement of a battle; but we may very well conceive that the effectual taking of this village forms, nevertheless, part of the destructive measure by which the enemy's force is to be shattered and reduced.

On the other hand, if we suppose an order given to a considerable Corps, perhaps a third or a half of the whole force, to take a certain important part of the enemy's position, then the result expected through this Corps may easily be so important as to be decisive for the whole; and if this Corps attains its object, no further decisive act may then be necessary. Now it is easy to conceive further that, owing to distance and the nature of the country, very few orders can be transmitted to this Corps in the course of the battle, consequently that both preparatory and decisive measures must be left to its discretion. In this manner one

[55] The larger and more dispersed a military force is, the more decentralized its command and control.

common decisive act falls to the ground altogether, and it is divided into separate decisive acts of some of the great parts.

(212) This, indeed, frequently takes place in great battles, and a pedantic notion of the *severance of the two acts* of which we conceive the battle to consist would therefore be in contradiction with the course of such a battle.

(213) Although we set up this distinction in the working of a battle as a point of great importance, it is far from *our intention* to place importance on the *regular severance and division* of these two activities, and to insist upon that as a practical principle; we only wish to separate in idea two things which are essentially different, and to show how this inherent difference governs of itself *the form of the combat.*

(214) The difference in the form shows itself most plainly in small combats, where the simple fire and close combat form a complete contrast to each other. The contrast is less decided when the parts are larger, because then in the two acts the two forms of combat from which they proceed unite themselves again; but the acts themselves are greater, take more time, and consequently are further separated from each other in time.

(215) There may be no separation also as regards the whole in so far that the decision has been already handed over to separate Corps of the first order; but still even then a trace of it will be found in the whole, as it must be our endeavour to bring the decisions of these different Corps into concert in relation to time, whether it be that we consider it necessary that the decisions should take place simultaneously, or that the decisions should take place in a certain order of succession.

(216) The difference between these two acts will, therefore, never be completely lost, as respects the whole, and that which is lost for the whole will reappear in the elements of the first order.

Notes

(217) This is the way in which our view is to be understood, and if thus understood, then, on the one hand, it will not come short of the reality, and on the other, it will direct the attention of the leader of a combat (let it be great or small, partial or general) to giving each of the two acts of activity its due share, that there may be neither precipitation nor negligence.

(218) *Precipitation* there will be if sufficient space and time are not allowed to the destructive act, if things are broken across the knee; an unfortunate issue of the decision results, which either cannot be repaired at all, or at all events remains a substantial disadvantage.[56]

(219) *Negligence* in general there will be if a complete decision does not take place, either from want of courage or from a wrong view of the situation; the result of this is always waste of force, but it may further be a positive disadvantage, because the maturity of the decision does not quite depend upon the duration of the destructive act, but on other circumstances as well, that is to say, on a favourable opportunity.

Plan of Battle—Definition[57]

(220a) The plan of the battle makes its unity possible; every action in common requires such unity. This unity is nothing else but the object of the combat; from it proceeds the directions which require to be given to all the different parts, in order to attain the object in the best way. The appointment of the object, and the arrangements consequent upon it, form therefore the plan.

(220b) We mean here, by plan, everything which is prescribed respecting the battle, whether beforehand, at the commencement, or in the course of the engagement; consequently, the whole operation of intelligence on matter.

(220c) But there is plainly an essential difference between such directions on the one hand, as must be and can be given previ-

[56] Clausewitz seems to be saying that if a plan of battle is rushed—if either executed too early or if a commander tries to do too much in too little time—the commander will be at a disadvantage.

[57] See *Marine Corps Planning Process*, Marine Corps Warfighting Publication (MCWP) 5-10 (formerly MCWP 5-1) (Washington, DC: Headquarters Marine Corps, 2016).

ously, and those, on the other hand, which the exigencies of the moment require.

(220d) The first constitutes the *Plan* in the proper sense, the latter we may call the *Conduct* (of the battle).[58]

(221) As these determinations which the moment calls forth are chiefly derived from the reciprocal action of the opposing parties, we shall leave the discussion and analysis of this difference until we come to the subject of the "reciprocal action."

(222) A part of the plan lies ready made in the formation (tactical organisation) of the combatant forces, by which the great number of parts is reduced to a few.

(223) In a partial combat this formation is a thing of more consequence than in the total combat; in the former it often constitutes the whole plan, and the smaller the body, the more this will be the case. A Battalion in a great battle does not use many other dispositions than those prescribed by the regulations and on the drill ground; but that is not sufficient for a Division, there particular directions become more necessary.

(224) But in the total combat the formation is seldom the whole plan, even for the smallest body: the plan often modifies the formation to afford scope for special dispositions. A Squadron undertaking the surprise of one of the enemy's small posts divides itself into several separate parts just as well as the largest Army.[59]

Aim of the Plan

(225) The object of the combat makes the unity of the plan; we may regard it as its aim, that is, the direction to which all activities should converge.[60]

[58] Here, Clausewitz is differentiating between planning and execution.

[59] Today, this is referred to as *task-organization*.

[60] The aim of the mission serves to unify the action of disparate units, combat arms, and staffs.

(226) The object of a combat is victory; in other words, everything which is a condition of victory, and which is included in No. 4.[61]

(227) None of the objects enumerated in No. 4 can be attained in battle, except by the destruction of the enemy's force, which, therefore, appears to be the means for all.

(228) It is itself in most cases the principal object as well.

(229) If that is the case the plan is aimed at the greatest possible destruction of the enemy's forces.[62]

(230) When some of the other things named in No. 1 are of greater importance than the destruction of the enemy's force, it takes a subordinate place as a means; then the greatest possible is no longer demanded, but only a sufficient destruction, and we may then take the nearest way to the aim.[63]

(231a) There are cases in which the points named in No. 4, *b*, *c*, *d*, *e*, *f*, which lead to the retreat of the enemy, may be attained without any destruction of the enemy's armed forces; then the enemy is conquered by a manœuvre and not by a combat. But this is no victory, therefore only for use when we have something else than a victory for an object.

(231b) In such cases, the employment of military force will still always imply the idea certainly of a combat, therefore of a destruction of the enemy's force, but only as *possible* not as *probable.* For inasmuch as our views are aimed at something else than the destruction of the enemy's forces, we pre-suppose these other things to be effectual, and that they will prevent any serious opposition from taking place. If we cannot make such a pre-supposition, then we ought not to choose these other things for our end, and if we err in the pre-supposition, the plan will miss its aim.

[61] (4) The enemy is moved to [evacuate the battlefield]:
    (a) If his loss is excessive,
        (i) . . . fears he will be overpowered,
        (ii) . . . the object will cost him too much.
    (b) . . . formation of his Army . . . is too much shaken.
    (c) . . . fear excessive loss if he continues the combat.
    (d) . . . order of battle is attended with too great disadvantages.
    (e) . . . taken by surprise . . . or suddenly attacked.
    (f) . . . perceives that his opponent is too superior.
    (g) . . . opponent has too great a superiority in moral forces.
As found on p. 30.

[62] Military thought has advanced since this time (231a). Maneuver warfare is a philosophy where victory is attained through other means.

[63] (1) What is the object of the combat?
    (a) Destruction of the enemy's armed forces.
    (b) To gain possession of some object.
    (c) Merely victory for the credit of our arms.
    (d) Two of these objects, or all three taken together.
As found on p. 30.

(232) From the preceding number it follows that whenever a considerable destruction of the enemy's forces is the condition of victory, it must also be the chief object of the plan.

(233) Now, as a manœuvre is not in itself a combat, but a combat takes place if a manœuvre does not succeed, therefore neither can the rules which apply to total combat suit the case of a manœuvre; and the particular things which are efficacious in a manœuvre can contribute nothing to the theory of the combat.

(234) Many mixed relations certainly arise in practice, but that is no reason against separating things in theory which in themselves are essentially different; if we know the nature of each part, then the combination of them may easily be made.

(235) The destruction of the enemy's armed force is, therefore, in all cases the aim, and the things named in No. 4, *b*, *c*, *d*, *e*, *f*, are first called forth by it, but then certainly enter into reciprocal action with it as powers in themselves.[64]

(236) Such of these things as perpetually recur—that is to say, are not the consequence of special relations—ought also properly to be regarded as effects of the destruction of the enemy's forces.

(237) So far, therefore, as it is possible to establish anything quite general as to the plan of a battle, it can only relate to the most effectual application of our own forces to the destruction of the enemy's.

Relation between the Magnitude and Certainty of the Result

(238) In War, and therefore, of course, in combat, we have to deal with moral forces and effects which cannot be nicely calculated; there must, consequently, always remain a great uncertainty as to the result of the means applied.[65]

[64] Here, Clausewitz contradicts himself, leaning more toward an attritionist mindset. These ideas are fleshed out in *On War*. See specifically Clausewitz, *On War*, vol. 1, book 1, chap. 2, 27–45.

[65] See *Warfighting* 7–9 for uncertainty and 15–17 for moral forces.

(239) This is still further increased by the number of contingencies with which operations in War are brought into contact.

(240) Wherever there is uncertainty, risk becomes an essential element.

(241) To *risk*, in the ordinary acceptation, means to build upon things which are more improbable than probable. *To risk*, in the widest sense, is to suppose things which are not certain. We shall take it here in the latter sense.

(242) Now, if there was in all cases a clearly defined line between probability and improbability, the idea might occur to us to make it the boundary-line of risk, and hold the passing of that line as inadmissible, that is, as risk in the restricted sense of the word.

(243) But, in the first place, such a line is a chimera; and, in the next, the combat is not an act of reflection only, but of passion and courage as well. These things cannot be shut out: if we should try to confine them too closely, we should divest our own powers of the most powerful springs of action in War, and involve ourselves in constant disadvantage; for in most cases the falling short of the (true) line, which is so unavoidable and frequent, is only compensated by our sometimes over-stepping it.

(244) The more favourable our pre-suppositions—that is to say, the greater the risk we run—so much the greater are the results which we expect by these same means, and therefore the objects which we have in view.

(245) The more we risk the less the probability and, consequently, the certainty of the result.

(246) The greatness of the result and the certainty of it stand, therefore, in opposition to each other when the means given are the same.

Notes

(247) The first question now is, how much value we should put upon one or other of these two opposite principles.

(248) Upon this nothing general can be laid down; on the contrary, of all questions in War it is the one most dependent on the particular circumstances in each case. In the first place, it is determined by relations which, in many cases, oblige us to run the greatest risks. Secondly, the spirit of enterprise and courage are things purely subjective, which cannot be prescribed. We can require of a Commander that he should judge of his means and relations with professional knowledge, and not overestimate their effects; if he does this, then we must trust to him to turn his means to the best advantage with the aid of his courage.

Relation between the magnitude of the result and the price[66]
(249) The second question in relation to the destruction of the enemy's forces concerns the price to be paid for it.

(250) With the intention of destroying the enemy's forces is certainly in general included the idea of destroying more than we shall in turn sacrifice on our own part; but this is by no means a necessary condition, for there may be cases (for instance, when we have a great superiority in numbers) when the mere diminution of the enemy's forces is an advantage, even if we pay for it by greater loss on our own side.

(251) But even if we aim decidedly at destroying more of the enemy's force than we sacrifice on our own side, still there always remains the question how great is that sacrifice to be, for according to it the chance of the result naturally rises and falls.

(252) We readily perceive that the answer to this question depends on the value which we place on our forces, therefore on individual interests. To these interests the decision must be left; and we can neither say that it is a rule to spare our own troops as much as possible, or to make a lavish use of them.

66 This is classic cost-benefit analysis.

Determination of the nature of combat for the separate parts (corps, &c.)

(253) The plan of the battle fixes for each single Division where, when, and how it is to fight—that is, it fixes *time*, *place*, and *form* of the combat.[67]

(254) Here, as well as everywhere, the general relations, that is, those proceeding from the abstract idea, are to be distinguished from those which the particular case brings with it.

(255) The manifold diversity in plans of battles must naturally proceed from the special relations in each case, because when the special advantages and disadvantages are sought for and discovered, the former are brought into use, and the latter are neutralised.

(256) But the general relations also give certain results, and although few in number and simple in form, still they are very important, because they belong to the very essence of the thing, and constitute the basis in all other decisions.

Attack and Defence[68]

(257) In regard to the nature of the combat there are only two distinctions, which always appear and are therefore general; the first arises from the positive or negative intention, and is the distinction between attack or defence; the other arises from the nature of arms, and is the distinction between the fire combat and the close combat.

(258) In the strictest sense, defence should only be the warding off a blow, and should therefore require no other weapon than a shield.

(259) But that would be a pure negation, a state absolutely passive; and making War is anything but patient endurance; the idea of thorough passivity can therefore never be laid at the root of defence.

[67] Today, this is referred to as *time, space,* and *forces,* and is generally a planning function of the operations staff.

[68] For the concepts of offense and defense, see *Warfighting*, 33–35, although the conception there is largely drawn from *On War*.

(260) Strictly considered, fire-arms, the most passive of weapons, have still something positive and active in their nature. Now the defence makes use, in general, of the same weapons, and also of the same forms of combat as the attack, both in fire and close combat.

(261) The defence is therefore to be considered a contest just as much as the attack.

(262) The object of this contest can be nothing but victory; which is, therefore, just as much an object for the defence as for the attack.

(263) There is nothing to justify the conception of the defender's victory being something negative; if somewhat like it, in certain cases, that lies in particular conditions: into the *conception* of the defence that notion *must* not enter, otherwise it reacts logically on the whole idea of combat, and introduces into it contradictions, or leads back again, by strict deduction, to that absurdity, a state of absolute endurance and sufferance.

(264) And yet there is a difference between attack and defence which, while it is the only one in principle, is also a very essential one; it is, that *the assailant wills the action* (*the combat*), *and calls it into life; whilst the defender waits for it.*

(265) This principle runs through all War, therefore through the whole province of combat, and in it all differences between attack and defence have their origin.

(266) But whoever wills an action must aim at something thereby, and this object must be something *positive*, because the intention *that nothing should be done* could call forth no action. The offensive must, therefore, have a *positive* object.

(267) Victory cannot be this object, for it is only a means. Even in a case where victory is sought entirely on account of itself, on ac-

Notes

count of the mere honour of arms, or to influence political nego-
tiations by its moral weight, still, that effect, and not the victory
itself, is always the object.[69]

(268) The defender, just as well as the aggressor, must have
victory in view, but in each the desire springs from a different
source; in the offensive from the object which the victory is to
serve; in the defender, from the mere fact of the combat. The one
looks down upon it, as it were, from a higher standpoint; the
other looks up to it from a lower position. Whoever fights can
only fight for the victory.

(269) Now, why does the defender fight, that is, why does he ac-
cept the combat? Because he will not concede the positive object
of the offensive; or, in other words, because he wants to maintain the *status quo*. This is the primary and necessary object of
the defender; whatever further may attach itself to this is not
necessary.

(270) The necessary intention of the defender, or rather the necessary part of the defender's intention, is therefore *negative*.

(271a) Wherever there is this negativity on the part of the defender, that is, wherever and whenever it is his interest that nothing
should be done, but that things should remain as they are, he is
thereby enjoined not to act, but to wait until his opponent acts;
but the moment that the latter acts, the defender can no longer
attain his object by waiting and not acting; he, therefore, now
acts just as well as his opponent, and the difference ceases.

(271b) If we apply this, in the first place, to the whole combat
only, then all difference between attack and defence will consist
in this, that the one waits for the other; but the course of the actual combat will not be further influenced by it.

(272) But this principle of the defence may also be applied to
partial combats: it may be for the interest of Corps, or parts of

[69] This is not a new definition of victory, but a further development of the concept. Victory is the object of combat until it is analyzed with respect to the offense and the defense. Once these two concepts are introduced, the concept of victory is modified to integrate them. Victory for the offense is not just winning but acquiring something thereby, such as territory. Victory for the defense is not just winning but retaining something thereby.

an Army, that no change should take place, and in that way they may also be led to adopt an attitude of expectation.

(273) This is not only possible as regards branches and Corps on the side of the defender, but also as respects those on the side of the assailant; it takes place in reality on both sides.

(274) It is natural, however, that it should occur more frequently in the case of the defender than in that of the assailant, but this can only be shown when the particular circumstances in connection with the defensive principle come under consideration.

(275) The more we imagine the defensive principle descending to the smallest branches in a total combat, and the more generally it is diffused throughout all the branches, so much the more passive becomes the whole resistance, so much the more the defence approaches to that point of absolute endurance which we look upon as an absurdity.

(276) The point in this direction at which the advantage to the defender of waiting ceases, that is, the point where its efficacy is exhausted, where, to a certain extent it is satiated, we shall only be able to examine closely hereafter.

(277) For the present, all that we deduce from what has been said is that the offensive or defensive intention not only determines something as to the commencement of the combat, but may also pervade its whole course—that by that means there are therefore in reality two different kinds of combat.

(278) The plan of the combat must therefore determine in every case whether as a whole it is to be an offensive or defensive combat.

(279) It must also determine this point for those Corps which have assigned to them a mission different from that of the general body.

Notes

(280) If we now leave out of consideration for the present every particular circumstance which might decide the choice of attack and defence, then there is only one rule which presents itself, namely, that *when we wish to defer the solution we must act defensively; when we seek it, offensively.*

(281) We shall see this principle come into connection presently with another which will make it plainer.

Fire Combat and Close Combat[70]
(282) The plan of the combat must further determine the choice of the form of combat in its relation to arms—that is, fire combat and close combat.

(283) But these two forms are not so much branches of the combat as essential elements of it. They result from the armament, they belong to each other, and only by the combination of the two together can the full power of the combat be developed.

(284) The truth of this view (which otherwise is not absolute but only approximative, comprehending the majority of cases), shows itself by the combination of arms in the hands of one combatant, and by the intimate union of different kinds of troops which has become a necessity.

(285) But a separation of these two elements and the use of the one without the other is not only possible, but very frequently happens.

(286) In respect to the mutual relations of the two, and their natural order amongst themselves, the plan of the battle has nothing to determine, as these are determined already by conception, by the formation (tactical organisation), and the drill-ground, and therefore, like the formation, belong to the stereotypic part of the plan.

[70] Here, Clausewitz is returning to the concepts of fire combat and close combat, this time as part of planning, which should determine how and when both should be employed.

(287) As to the use of these two forms of combat apart from each other, there is no general rule, unless this can pass for such, that such separation must always be regarded as a necessary evil, that is, as a less effective form of action. All cases in which we are obliged to make use of this weaker form belong to the domain of particular circumstances. Occasions for the use of the bayonet alone, such, for instance, as the execution of a surprise, or when there is no time to use fire-arms, or if we are sure of a great superiority of courage on our side are plainly only isolated cases.

Determination of Time and Place[71]

(288) As to the determination of time and place, we have, in the first place, to observe in reference to these two things, that in the total combat the determination of place belongs to the defence alone, the determination of time to the attack.

(289) But for partial combats, the plan either of an offensive or of a defensive combat has to give determinations respecting both.

Time

(290) The appointment of time for a partial combat, which seems at first sight only to affect the subject at most in a few points, takes, however, a different turn on closer examination, and is seen to penetrate it through and through with a ruling idea, decisive in the highest degree, that is, the possibility of a successive use of forces.

Successive Use of Forces

(291) Simultaneous action is, in itself, a fundamental condition of the common action of separate forces. This is also the case in War, and particularly in the combat. For as the number of the combatants is a factor in the product of the same, therefore, *ceteris paribus*, the simultaneous application of all our forces, that is, the greatest assemblage of them in time against an enemy who does not employ all his at once, will give the victory, certainly in the first instance only, over that part of the enemy's force which has been employed; but as this victory over a part of the enemy's

[71] This correlation between time and space with respect to offense and defense is more developed than in *On War* because it is a tactical consideration. Defense chooses where to defend, but the offense chooses when to attack. An offensive-defense uses elements of the offense (e.g., patrols) to challenge the attacker's control of time, by throwing off their timing.

forces raises the moral force of the conqueror, and lowers that of the vanquished, it follows, therefore, that although the loss of physical force may be equal on both sides, still this *partial victory* has the effect of raising the total forces of the conqueror and diminishing those of the vanquished, and that consequently it may determine the result of the total combat.[72]

(292) But the deduction drawn in the preceding number supposes two conditions which do not exist; in the first place, that the number (of troops) must have no maximum; and, secondly, that the use of one and the same force has no limits as long as there is anything left of it.

(293) As regards the first of these points, the number of combatants is limited at once by space, for all that cannot be brought into actual use are superfluous. By it the depth and extent of the formation of all combatants intended to act simultaneously is limited, and consequently the number of combatants.[73]

(294) But a much more important limitation of numbers lies in the nature of the fire combat. We have seen (No. 89c) that in it, within certain limits, the increase of number has only the effect of raising the strength of the fire combat on both sides; that is, its total effects. Now this increased effect, when it brings no advantage in itself for one side, ceases then to be of service to that side; it therefore easily reaches a maximum in that case.[74]

(295) This maximum determines itself entirely by the individual case, by the ground, the moral relations between the opposing troops, and the more immediate object of the fire combat. Here it is enough to say that there is such a thing.

(296) The number of troops to be employed simultaneously has, therefore, a maximum, beyond which a waste takes place.

(297) In the same way the use of one and the same body of troops has its limits. We have seen (in No. 123) how troops under fire

[72] *Ceteris paribus* means, in Latin, "all other conditions being the same."

[73] This is a very practical observation. While it remains true, the space in which we operate now includes cyberspace, the electromagnetic spectrum, and the informational domain. The space of these domains is still limited physically, though not in the same dimensions of height, width, and depth.

[74] (89c) We may, therefore, say that either of the opposing sides has it in his power to increase or reduce the mutual, that is, the total effect of the fire, according as he brings or does not bring more combatants into the line which is firing. As found on p. 58.

gradually become unserviceable; but there is likewise a deterioration in close combat. The exhaustion of physical force is less there than in fire combat, but the moral effect produced by an unsuccessful issue is infinitely greater.[75]

(298) Through this deterioration, which forces used in action suffer, including as well those not actually engaged, a new principle comes into the combat, which is the inherent superiority of fresh troops opposed to those already used.

(299) There is still a second subject for consideration, which consists in a temporary deterioration of forces that have been engaged in the crisis which occurs in every action.

(300) The close combat in practice may be said to have no duration. In the moment that the shock takes place between two cavalry regiments the thing is decided, and the few seconds of actual sword-fight are of no consequence as regards time: it is very much the same with infantry and with large masses. But the affair is not then finished on that account; the state of crisis which has burst out with the decision is not yet quite over; the victorious Regiment pursuing the vanquished at full speed is not the same Regiment lately drawn up on the field of battle in perfect order; its moral force is certainly intensified, but, as a rule, its physical force, as well as that resulting from military order in its ranks, has suffered. It is only by the loss which his adversary has suffered in moral strength, and by the circumstance that he is just as much disordered, that the conqueror retains his superiority, therefore, if a new adversary makes his appearance with his moral force intact, and his ranks in perfect order, there can be no question that, supposing the troops equally good, he will beat the conqueror.

(301) A similar crisis also takes place in the fire combat, to such a degree that the side which has just been victorious by its fire, and has driven back its enemy, still finds itself, for the moment, in a decidedly weakened condition as respects order in its ranks,

[75] (123) After a fire combat of several hours' duration, in which a body of troops has suffered severe loss, for instance, a quarter or one-third of its numbers, the *débris* may, for the time, be looked upon as a heap of burnt-out cinders, for—

   (a) The men are physically exhausted.
   (b) They have spent their ammunition.
   (c) Their arms want cleaning.
   (d) Many have left the field with the wounded, although not themselves wounded.
   (e) The rest think they have done their part for the day, and if once they get beyond the sphere of danger do not willingly return to it.
   (f) The feeling of courage with which they started has had the edge taken off, the longing for the fight is satisfied.
   (g) The original organisation and formation are partly destroyed, or thrown into disorder.

As found on p. 70.

and physical and moral force, a condition which lasts until all that has been thrown into disorder is once more restored to its normal relations.

(302) What we have said here of smaller units holds good with respect to larger ones as well.

(303) The crisis is in itself greater in smaller units, because it has an effect uniformly throughout the whole, but it is of shorter duration.

(304) The weakest is a general crisis, especially of a whole Army; but it lasts the longest in large Armies, often for several hours.

(305) As long as the conqueror is in the crisis of the combat, the conquered has in that crisis a means of still restoring the combat, that is, of turning its result, if he can bring forward fresh troops in sufficient numbers.

(306) In this manner, therefore, the successive employment of troops is introduced in a second way, as an efficacious principle.

(307) But if the successive employment of troops in a series of combats following one after another is possible; and if the simultaneous use is not unlimited, then it follows of itself that the forces, which cannot be efficacious in simultaneous action, may become so in successive efforts.

(308) By this series of partial combats, *one after another*, the duration of the whole combat is considerably extended.

(309) This duration now brings into view a fresh motive for the successive use of forces, by introducing a new quantity into the calculation, which is *the unforeseen event*.[76]

(310) If, in general, a successive use of troops is possible, then it follows that we can no longer know how the enemy will employ

[76] While the idea of "the unforeseen event" highlights the role of uncertainty in war, the practical application, for Clausewitz, is the use of the reserve. See Clausewitz, *On War*, vol. 1, book 3, chap. 13, 217–20.

his; for only that portion which is brought into action at once comes within the scope of our observation, the rest does not, and therefore we can only form some general conjectures respecting it.

(311) By the mere duration of the action there is brought into our reckoning an increased amount of pure chance, and that element naturally plays a more important part in War than anywhere else.

(312) Unforeseen events require a general system of precaution, and this can consist in nothing else than placing in rear a proportionate force, which is the reserve, properly speaking.

Depth of the Order of Battle

(313) All battles which are to be fought by bodies of troops in succession require from their very nature that fresh troops should be forthcoming. These may either be quite fresh, that is, troops which have not been engaged at all, or such as have been in action, but by rest have recovered more or less from their exhaustion. It is easy to see that this gives room for many shades of difference.

(314) Both the use of quite fresh troops as well as the use of such as have refreshed themselves supposes that they have been in rear—that is, in a position beyond the region of destruction.

(315) This also has its degrees, for the region of destruction does not end at once, but decreases gradually until at last it ends entirely.

(316) The range of small arms and of grape are well-defined gradations.[77]

(317) The further a body of troops is posted in rear, the fresher they will be when brought into action.

[77] *Grape* refers to *grapeshot*, a kind of artillery round that is a collection of smaller projectiles packed tightly into some kind of casing, like a canvas bag, to form a cannister. When fired, the projectiles would spread out and cause more damage to unprotected targets. It was more effective than cannonballs against infantry and cavalry forces at close range.

(318) But no body of troops which has been within reach of an effective fire of small arms, or of case, can be considered fresh.

(319) We have, therefore, three reasons for keeping a certain number of troops in rear. They serve (a) to relieve or reinforce exhausted troops, especially in fire combat.
    (b) To profit by the crisis in which the conqueror is placed directly after his success.
    (c) As a provision against unforeseen events.

(320) All troops kept back come under these categories whatever arm they belong to, whether we call them a second line or reserve, whether they are part of a Division, or of the whole.

Polarity of the Simultaneous and Successive Use of Troops[78]

(321) As the simultaneous and the successive use of troops are opposed to one another, and each has its advantages, they may be regarded as two poles, each of which attracts the resolution to itself, and by that means fixes it at a point where they are in a state of equilibrium, provided that this resolution is founded on a right estimate of the opposing forces.

(322) Now, we require to know the laws of this polarity—that is, the advantages and conditions of these two applications of force, and thereby also their relations with one another.

(323) The simultaneous employment of forces may be intensified—
    A. With equal fronts—both
        (a) In fire combat.
        (b) In close combat.
    B. With a greater front, that is, enveloping.

(324) Only those forces which are brought into efficient activity at the same time can be regarded as applied simultaneously. When the fronts are equal, such application is therefore limited by the possibility of acting effectively. For instance, in fire com-

[78] Here, Clausewitz is referring to the concentrated use of all available forces in time (simultaneous) or the use of available troops in waves or phases (successive). Both methods have advantages and disadvantages.

bat, three ranks might perhaps fire at the same time, but six cannot.

(325) We have shown (in No. 89) that two lines of fire of *unequal* strength as regards numbers may be a match for each other, and that a diminution (of numbers) on one side, if it does not exceed certain limits, has only the result of *reducing the mutual effect*.[79]

(326) But the more the destructive effect of the fire combat is diminished, the more time is required to produce the necessary effect. Therefore, that side which desires chiefly to gain time (commonly the defensive side) is interested in modifying, as much as possible, the total destructive effect of the fire (that is, the sum of the mutual fire).

(327) Further, this must also be an object with the side which is much the weaker in point of numbers, because, when the losses are equal, his are always relatively greatest.

(328) When the conditions are reversed, the interests will be reversed also.

(329) When no special interest for hastening the action predominates, it will be the interest of both sides to do with as few troops as possible, that is, as already said (No. 89b), only to employ so many that the enemy will not be induced to come to close quarters at once, owing to the smallness of our numbers.[80]

(330) In this manner, therefore, the simultaneous employment of forces in fire combat is limited by the *want of any advantage*, and both sides have to fall back upon the successive use of the spare forces.

(331) In close combat the superiority in numbers is above all things decisive, and the *simultaneous* employment of troops is on that account so much to be preferred to the *successive*, that the

[79] (89a) *Superiority of numbers.* As found on p. 56.

[80] (89b) Economy of force. As found on p. 58.

latter in mere theory is almost completely excluded, and only becomes possible through accessory circumstances.

(332) Close combat is in fact a decision, and one which lasts hardly any time; this excludes the successive use of forces.

(333) But we have already said that the crisis of the close combat affords favourable scope for the successive use of forces.

(334) Further, the decisions in partial close combats belonging to a greater whole are not absolute decisions; therefore the application of our force to the further combats which are possible must also be taken into consideration.

(335) This leads then also to not using at one time more troops in close combat than appear to be just necessary to make certain of the result.

(336) As regards this point there is no other general rule, except that circumstances which obstruct execution (such as a very courageous enemy, difficult ground, &c.) occasion a necessity for a greater number of troops.

(337) But for the general theory, it is of consequence to observe that the employment of more troops than is necessary in close combat is never so disadvantageous as in fire combat, because in the first, the troops only become unserviceable at the time of the crisis, not for a continuance.

(338) The simultaneous employment of forces in the close combat is therefore subject to this rule, that it must in all cases be sufficient to produce the result, and that the successive use can in no way make up for insufficiency, for the results cannot be added together as in fire combat; and further, that when once the point of sufficiency is reached, any greater simultaneous application of force becomes a waste of power.

Notes

(339) Now that we have considered the application of large bodies of troops in fire and close combat, by increasing the depth of the same, we come to that which is possible by *extending the front*, that is, in the enveloping form.[81]

(340) There are two ways in which we may conceive a greater number of combatants brought simultaneously into action through a greater width of front, viz.:[82]
   (a) By extending our front so as to cause the enemy to extend his also. This does not give us any superiority over the enemy, but it has the effect of bringing more forces into play on both sides.
   (b) By outflanking the enemy's front.

(341) To bring more forces into action on both sides can in very few cases be of any advantage to one of the two sides, it is also uncertain whether the enemy will respond to this further extension of front.

(342) If he does not respond, then a part of our front, that is of our forces, will be either unemployed, or we must apply the overlapping part of our front to *turn* the enemy.

(343) It is then only the apprehension of this turning which moves the enemy to extend as far as we have done.

(344) If, however, the enemy is to be turned, it is plainly better to make arrangements for that purpose from the first, and therefore we should consider an extension of front only from that point of view.

(345) Now, in the employment of troops, the enveloping form has this peculiar property, that it not only increases the number of troops simultaneously engaged on the two sides, but it also allows us (the party using it) to bring more of them into activity than the enemy can.

[81] See *Marine Corps Operations*, chap. 9, specifically "Forms of Maneuver," 9-9–9-17, for more on flanking, envelopment, and other such tactics.

[82] The abbreviation *viz.* stands for the Latin phrase *videre licet*, which means "it is permitted to see."

(346) If, for instance, a Battalion with a front 180 paces in length is surrounded, and has to show front on four sides, and if the enemy is at a distance of musketry range, (150 yards) from it, then there would be room for eight Battalions to act with effect against that single Battalion.

(347) The enveloping form therefore comes in here on account of this peculiarity; but we must at the same time bring under consideration its other specialities also, that is, its advantages and disadvantages.

(348) A second advantage of the enveloping form is the increased effect resulting from the concentration of fire.

(349) A third advantage is its effect in the interception of the enemy's retreat.

(350) These three advantages of enveloping diminish according as the forces, or rather their fronts, become greater, and they increase the smaller the fronts are.

(351) For as regards the first (No. 345), the range of arms remains the same, whether the masses of troops be great or small (it being understood that they consist of the same arms of the service), the actual difference, therefore, between the enveloping line and the line enveloped is a quantity which always remains the same; and, consequently, its relative value is always diminishing in proportion as the front is extended.

(352) To surround a Battalion, at 150 yards, eight Battalions are required (No. 346); but ten Battalions, on the other hand, might be surrounded by only twenty Battalions.

(353) The enveloping form, however, is seldom, if ever, carried out *completely*, that is to say, to the complete circle, rarely more than partially, and usually within 180°. Now, if we imagine to ourselves a body of the size of a considerable Army, we see plain-

Notes

ly how little will remain of the first of the above advantages under such circumstances.

(354) It is just the same with the second advantage, as may be seen at a glance.

(355) The third advantage, also, of course, notably diminishes by the greater extension of the front; although, here, some other relations also come into consideration.

(356) But the enveloping form has also a peculiar disadvantage, which is, that the troops being, by that form, spread out over a greater space, their efficient action is diminished in two respects.

(357) For instance, the time which is required to go over a certain space cannot, at the same time, be utilised for fighting. Now, all movements which do not lead perpendicularly on the enemy's line have to be made over a greater space by the enveloping party than by the party enveloped, because the latter moves more or less on the radii of the smaller circle, the former on the circumference of the greater, which makes an important difference.

(358) This gives the side enveloped the advantage of a greater facility in the use of his forces at *different* points.

(359) But the unity of the whole is also lessened by the greater space covered, because intelligence and orders must pass over greater distances.[83]

(360) Both these disadvantages of enveloping increase with the increase in the width of front. When there are only a few Battalions they are insignificant; with large Armies, on the other hand, they become important—for

(361) The difference between radius and circumference is constant; therefore, the absolute difference becomes always greater,

[83] Information is a product of the medium in which it travels and also takes time to travel greater distances.

the greater the front becomes; and it is with absolute differences we are now concerned.

(362) Besides, with quite small bodies of troops few or no flank movements occur, whilst they become more frequent as the size of the masses increases.

(363) Lastly, as regards interchange of communications, there is no difference as long as the whole space is only such as can be overlooked.

(364) Therefore, if the advantages of the enveloping form are very great and the disadvantages very small when the fronts are short; if the advantages diminish and the disadvantages increase with the extension of front, it follows that there must be a point where there is an equilibrium.

(365) Beyond that point, therefore, the extension of front can no longer offer any advantages over the successive use of troops; but, on the contrary, disadvantages arise.

(366) The equilibrium between the advantages of the successive use of forces, and those of a greater extent of front (No. 341) must, therefore, be on this side of that point.[84]

(367) In order to find out this point of equilibrium, we must bring the advantages of the enveloping form more distinctly into view. The simplest way to do so is as follows:

(368) A certain front is necessary in order to exempt ourselves from the effect of the first of the two disadvantages of being surrounded.

(369) As respects the convergent (double) effect of fire, there is a length of front where that completely ceases, namely, if the distance between the portions of the line bent back, in case we are surrounded by the enemy, exceeds that of the range of fire-arms.

84 (341) To bring more forces into action on both sides can in very few cases be of any advantage to one of the two sides, it is also uncertain whether the enemy will respond to this further extension of front. As found on p. 140.

(370) But, in rear of every position, a space out of reach of fire is required for the reserves, for those who command, &c., whose place is in rear of the front. If these were exposed to fire from three sides, then they could no longer fulfil the objects for which they are intended.

(371) As these details of themselves form considerable masses in large Armies, and, consequently, require more room, therefore, the greater the whole, the greater must be the space out of the reach of fire in rear of the front. Accordingly, on this ground, the front must increase as the masses increase.

(372) But the space (out of fire) behind a considerable mass of troops must be greater, not only because the reserves, &c., occupy more space, but, besides that also, in order to afford greater security; for, in the first place, the effect of stray shots would be more serious amongst large masses of troops and military trains than amongst a few Battalions; secondly, the combats of large masses last much longer, and, through that, the losses are much greater amongst the troops behind the front who are not actually engaged in the combat.

(373) If, therefore, a certain length is fixed for the necessary extent of front, then it must increase with the size of the masses.

(374) The other advantage of the enveloping form (the superiority in the number acting simultaneously) leads to no determinate quantity for the front of a line; we must therefore confine ourselves to saying that it diminishes with the extension of front.

(375) Further, we must point out that the simultaneous action of superior numbers here spoken of chiefly relates to *musketry fire*; for as long as artillery alone is in action, space will never be wanting, even for the enveloped on his smaller curve to plant as many pieces as the enemy can on the greater curve; because there never is enough artillery with an Army to cover the whole front of a continuous line.

Notes

(376) It cannot be objected that the enemy has still always an advantage in the greater space, because his guns need not stand so close, and therefore are less liable to be struck; for Batteries cannot be thus evenly distributed by single guns at equal intervals over a great space.

(377) In a combat of artillery alone, or in one in which the artillery plays the principal part, the greater extent of the enveloping front gives an advantage, and a great one too, through the great range of artillery, because that makes a great difference in the extent of the two fronts. This case occurs, for example, with single redoubts. But with Armies in which the other arms of the service take the most prominent part, and artillery only a secondary part, there is not this advantage, because, as already said, there is never any want of space even for the side enveloped.

(378) It is, therefore, principally in infantry combats that the advantage which the greater front affords of bringing greater numbers into action simultaneously must show itself. The difference of the two fronts in such a case amounts to three times the range of the musket (if the envelopment reaches an angle of 180°), that is, about 600 paces. Before a front of 600 paces in length, the enveloping line will then be double, which will be sensibly felt; but before a front of 3,000 paces the additional length would only be one-fifth, which is no advantage of any importance.

(379) We may say, therefore, respecting this point, that the length of front is sufficient as soon as the difference resulting from the range of a musket shot ceases to give the enveloping line any very marked superiority.

(380) From what has just been said of the two advantages of enveloping, it follows *that small masses have a difficulty in obtaining the requisite development of front*; this is so true that we know for a fact that they are in most cases obliged to give up their regular order of formation and to extend much more. It rarely happens that a single Battalion, if left to depend on itself, will engage in a

Notes

combat without extending its front beyond the ordinary length (150 and 200 paces); instead of keeping to that formation it will divide into companies with intervals between them, then again will extend into skirmishers, and after a part is placed in reserve it will take up with the rest, altogether twice, three or four times as much room as it should do normally.

(381) But the greater the masses the easier it is to attain the necessary extension of front, as the front increases with the masses (No. 373), although *not in the same proportion*.[85]

(382) Great masses have, therefore, no necessity to depart from their order of formation, on the contrary, they are able to place troops in rear.

(383) The consequence of this is, that for large masses a kind of standing formation has been introduced, in which portions of the force are drawn up in rear; such is the ordinary order of battle in two lines; usually there is a third one behind, consisting of cavalry, and besides that, also a reserve of one-eighth to one-sixth, &c.

(384) With very large masses (Armies of 100,000 to 150,000 or 200,000) we see the reserves always get greater (one-quarter to one-third), a proof that Armies have a continual tendency to increase further beyond what is required for the extent of front.

(385) We only introduce this now to show more plainly the truth of our demonstration by a glance at facts.

(386) Such, then, is the bearing of the first two advantages of enveloping. It is different with the third.

(387) The first two influence the *certainty* of the result by intensifying our forces, the third does that also, but only with very short fronts.

[85] (373) If, therefore, a certain length is fixed for the necessary extent of front, then it must increase with the size of the masses. As found on p. 148.

(388) It acts particularly on the courage of those engaged in the front of the enemy's line by creating a fear of losing their line of retreat, an idea which has always a great influence on soldiers.

(389) This is, however, only the case when the danger of being cut off is so imminent and evident that the impression overpowers all restraints of discipline and of authority, and carries away the soldier involuntarily.

(390) At greater distances, and if the soldier is only led to a sense of danger indirectly by the sound of artillery and musketry in his rear, uneasy feelings may arise within him, but, unless his spirit is already very bad, these will not prevent his obeying the orders of his superiors.

(391) In this case, therefore, the advantage in cutting off the enemy's retreat, which appertains to the enveloping side, cannot be regarded as one which makes success more *secure*, that is, more *probable*, but only as one which *increases* the *extent* of a success already commenced.

(392) In this respect, also, the third advantage of enveloping is subject to the counter-principle, that it is greatest with a short front, and decreases with the extension of front, as is evident.

(393) But this does not set aside the principle that greater masses should have a greater extent of front than small ones, because as a retreat is never made in the whole width of a position, but by certain roads, so it follows of itself that great masses require more time for a retreat than small ones; this longer time therefore imposes the necessity of a larger front, that the enemy who envelops this front may not so speedily gain the points through which the line of retreat passes.

(394) If (in accordance with No. 391) the third advantage of enveloping, in the majority of cases (that is, when the fronts are not too short), only influences the extent, but not the certainty,

Notes

of success, then it follows that it will have a very different value, according to the relations and views of the combatants.

(395) When the probability of the result is otherwise small, the first consideration must be to increase the probability; in such a case, therefore, an advantage which relates principally to the extent of the result cannot be of much consequence.

(396) But if this advantage is quite opposed (No. 565) to the probability of success, in such case it becomes a positive disadvantage.[86]

(397) In such a case, endeavour must be made, through the advantage of the successive use of forces, to counterbalance those of the greater extent of front.

(398) We see, therefore, that the point of indifference (or equilibrium) between the two poles of the *simultaneous* and *successive* application of our forces—of *extension of front* and *depth of position*—is differently situated, not only according as the masses are large or small, but also according to the relations and intentions of the respective parties.

(399) The weaker and the more prudent will give the preference to the successive use, the stronger and the bold to the simultaneous employment of the forces.

(400) It is natural that the assailant should be the *stronger*, or the *bolder*, whether from the character of the Commander or from necessity.

(401) The enclosing form of combat, or that form which implies the simultaneous use of forces on both sides in the highest degree, is, therefore, natural to the assailant.

[86] (565) This difference of circumstances consists in three things in particular, namely, in the want of data, in the want of time, and in danger. As found on p. 206.

(402) The enclosed, that is, one limited to the successive application of forces, and which, on that account, is in danger of being surrounded, is, therefore, the natural form of the defensive.

(403) In the first there is the tendency to a quick solution, in the latter to gain time, and these tendencies are in harmony with the object of each form of combat.

(404) But in the nature of the defensive there lies still another motive, which inclines it to the deeper order of battle.

(405) One of its most considerable advantages is the assistance of the country and ground, and local defence of the same constitutes an important element of this advantage.

(406) Now one would think this should lead to the front being made as wide as possible, in order to make the most of this advantage; a one-sided view, which may be regarded as the chief cause of Commanders having been so often led to occupy extensive positions.

(407) But hitherto we have always supposed the extension of front as either causing the enemy to extend, in like manner, or as leading to *outflanking*, that is, to an envelopment of the enemy's front.

(408) As long as we imagine both sides equally active, therefore apart from the point of view of offensive and defensive, the application of a more extended front to envelop the enemy presents no difficulty.

(409) But as soon as we combine more or less local defence with the combat in front (as is done in the defensive), then that application of the overlapping portions of the front ceases; it is either impossible, or very difficult, to combine local defence with outflanking.

Notes

(410) In order rightly to appreciate this difficulty, we must always bear in mind the form which the case assumes in reality when our view of an enemy's measures is intercepted by the natural means of cover which the ground affords, and therefore troops employed to defend any particular locality may be easily deceived and held in inactivity.

(411) From this it follows, that in the defensive it is to be considered a decided disadvantage to occupy a greater front than that which the enemy necessarily requires for the deployment of his forces.

(412) The necessary extent of front for the offensive we shall examine hereafter; here we have only to observe, that if the offensive takes up too narrow a front, the defensive does not punish him for it, through having made his own front wide at first, but *by an offensive enveloping counter-movement.*

(413) It is, therefore, certain that the defender, in order that he may not, in any case, incur the disadvantage of too wide a front, will always take up the narrowest which circumstances will permit, for by that means he can place the more troops in reserve; at the same time these reserves are never likely to be left inactive, like portions of a too extended front.[87]

(414) As long as the defender is satisfied with the narrowest front, and seeks to preserve the greatest depth, that is to say, as long as he follows the natural tendency of his form of combat, in the same degree there will be an opposite tendency on the part of the assailant; he will make the extent of his front as *great* as possible, or, in other words, envelop his enemy as far as possible.

(415) But this is a *tendency*, and no *law*; for we have seen that the advantages of this envelopment diminish with the lengths of the fronts; and therefore, at certain points, no longer counterbalance the advantage of the successive application of force. To this law the assailant is subject as well as the defender.

.

[87] Here, Clausewitz has his own version of "it depends": "which circumstances will permit."

(416) Now, here we have to consider extension of front of two kinds; that which the defender fixes by the position which he takes up, and that which the assailant is obliged to adopt with a view to outflanking his enemy.

(417) If the extension in the first case is so great that all the advantages of outflanking vanish or become ineffective, then that movement must be given up; the assailant must then seek to gain an advantage in another way, as we shall presently see.

(418) But if the defenders' front is as small as can possibly be, if the assailant, at the same time, has a right to look for advantages by outflanking and enveloping, still, again, the limits of this envelopment must be fixed.

(419) This limit is determined by the disadvantages inherent in any enveloping movement which is carried too far (Nos. 356 and 365).[88]

(420) These disadvantages arise when the envelopment is attempted against a front exceeding the length which would justify the movement; but they are evidently very much greater if the fault consists in too wide an envelopment of a short line.

(421) When the assailant has these disadvantages against him, then the advantages of the enemy in the successive employment of force through his short line must tell with more weight.

(422) Now, it certainly appears that the defender who adopts the narrow front and deep order of battle does not thereby retain all the advantages of the successive use of forces on his side: for if the assailant adopts a front as small, and, therefore, does not outflank his enemy, then it is possible for both equally to resort to the successive use of their forces; but if the assailant envelops his opponent, then the latter must oppose a front in every direction in which he is threatened, and, therefore, fight with the same extent of front (except the trifling difference between the

[88] (356) But the enveloping form has also a peculiar disadvantage, which is, that the troops being, by that form, spread out over a greater space, their efficient action is diminished in two respects. (365) Beyond that point, therefore, the extension of front can no longer offer any advantages over the successive use of troops; but, on the contrary, disadvantages arise. As found on pp. 144 and 146.

extent of concentric circles, which is not worth noticing). With respect to this there are four points which claim our attention.

(423) In the first place, let the assailant contract his front as much as he pleases, there is always an advantage for the defender in the combat changing from the form of one in extended order and which will be quickly decided into one which is concentrated and prolonged, for the prolongation of the combat is in favour of the defensive.

(424) Secondly, the defender, even if enveloped by his adversary, is not always obliged to oppose a parallel front to each of the Divisions surrounding him; he may attack them in flank or rear, for which the geometrical relations are just those which afford the best opportunity; but this is at once a successive use of forces, for in that it is not at all a necessary condition that the troops employed later should be employed exactly as the first used, or that the last brought forward should take up the ground occupied by the first, as we shall see presently more plainly. Without placing troops in reserve it would not be possible to *envelop the enveloping force* in this manner.

(425) Thirdly, by the short front, with strong reserves in rear, there is a possibility of the enemy carrying his enveloping movement too far (No. 420), of which advantage may then be taken, just by means of the forces placed in rear in reserve.

(426) Fourthly, in the last place, there is an advantage to the defender in being secured by this means against the opposite error of a waste of force, through portions of the front not being attacked.

(427) These are the advantages of a deep order of battle, that is, of the successive employment of forces. They not only check over-extension on the part of the defender, but also stop the assailant from overstepping certain limits in enveloping; without, however, stopping the tendency to extend within these limits.

Notes

(428) But this tendency will be weakened or completely done away with if the defender has extended himself too far.

(429) Under these circumstances certainly the defender, being deficient in masses in reserve, cannot punish the assailant for his too great extension in his attempt to envelop, but the advantages of the envelopment are, as it is, too small in such a case.

(430) The assailant will, therefore, now no longer seek the advantages of enveloping if his relations are not such that cutting off is a point of great importance to him. In this way, therefore, the tendency to enveloping is diminished.

(431) But it will be entirely done away with if the defender has taken up a front of such extent that the assailant can leave a great part of it inactive, for that is to him a decided gain.

(432) In such cases, the assailant ceases to look for advantages in extension and developing, and looks for them in the opposite direction, that is, in the concentration of his forces against some one point. It is easy to perceive that this signifies the same as a deep order of battle.

(433) How far the assailant may carry the contraction of the front of his position, depends on—
    (a) The size of the masses,
    (b) The extent of the enemy's front, and
    (c) His state of preparation to assume a counter-offensive.

(434) With small forces it is disadvantageous to leave any part of the enemy's front inactive; for, as the spaces are small, everything can be seen, and such parts can on the instant be applied to active purposes elsewhere.

(435) From this follows of itself, that also with larger masses and fronts the front attacked must not be too small, because otherwise the disadvantage just noticed would arise, at least partially.

Notes

(436) But, in general, it is natural that when the assailant has good reason to seek for his advantage in a concentration of his forces, on account of the excessive extension of front, or the passivity of the defender, he can go further in contracting the extent of his front than the defender, because the latter, through the too great extension of his front, is not prepared for an offensive counteraction against the enveloping movement.

(437) The greater the front of the defender, the greater will be the number of its parts which the assailant can leave unassailed.

(438) The same will be the case the more the intention of local defensive is distinctly pronounced;

(439) And, lastly, the greater the masses are generally.

(440) The assailant will therefore find the most advantage in a concentration of his forces if all these favourable circumstances are combined, namely, large masses, too long a front, and a great deal of local defence on the part of the enemy.

(441) This subject cannot be finished until we examine the relations of space.

(442) We have already shown (No. 291) the use of the successive employment of forces. We have only here to call the attention of our readers to the point that the motives for it relate not only to the renewal of the *same combat* with fresh troops, but also to every subsequent (or ulterior) employment of reserve troops.[89]

(443) In this *subsequent* use, there is *supreme advantage*, as will be seen in the sequel.

(444) From the preceding exposition, we see that the point where the simultaneous and the successive use of troops balance each other is different, according to the *mass of troops in reserve,*

[89] (291) Simultaneous action is, in itself, a fundamental condition of the common action of separate forces. This is also the case in War, and particularly in combat. For as the number of the combatants is a factor in the product of the same, therefore, *ceteris paribus* [all things being equal], the simultaneous application of all our forces, that is, the greatest assemblage of them in time against an enemy who does not employ all his at once, will give the victory, certainly in the first instance only, over that part of the enemy's force which has been employed; but as this victory over a part of the enemy's forces raises the moral force of the conqueror, and lowers that of the vanquished, it follows, therefore, that although the loss of physical forces may be equal on both sides, still this *partial victory* has the effect of raising the total forces of the conqueror and diminishing those of the vanquished, and that consequently it may determine the result of the total combat. As found on p. 124.

according to the *proportion of Force*, according to *situation* and *object*, according to *Boldness* and *Prudence*.

(445) That country and ground have likewise a great influence, is, of course, understood, and it only receives this bare mention, because all application is here left out of sight.

(446) With such manifold connections and complex relations, no absolute numbers can be fixed as normal quantities; but there must still be some unit which serves as a fixed point for these complex changeable relations.

(447) Now there are two such guides, one on each side first a certain depth, which allows of the simultaneous action of all the forces, may be looked upon as one guide. To reduce this depth for the sake of increasing the extension of front must therefore be regarded as a necessary evil. This, therefore, determines the *necessary depth*. The second guide is the security of the reserve, of which we have already spoken. This determines *the necessary extension*.

(448) The necessary depth just mentioned lies at the foundation of all standing formations; we shall not be able to prove this until hereafter, when we come to treat specially of the order of the (three) arms.

(449) But before we can bring our general considerations to a final conclusion, in anticipation of the above result, we must inquire into the determination of place, as that has some influence upon it likewise.

Determination of Place[90]
(450) The determination of place answers the question where the combat is to be, as well for the whole as for the parts.

(451) The place of combat for the whole emanates from Strategy, with which we are not now concerned. We have only here to deal

[90] These sections represent Clausewitz at his most rules-based, linear, and scientific; an outlook he rejected later. However, for instance, (see proposition 446, p. 170), which notes the "complex changeable relations," shows how Clausewitz was wrestling with the historical tendency to prescribe warfare, most often emblematic of Dietrich Adam Heinrich von Bülow's theories, with the reality of war, as he experienced it.

with the construction of the combat; we must, therefore, suppose that both parties have come into contact, the place of the combat will then generally be either where the enemy's Army is (*in the attack*), or where we can wait for it (*on the defensive*).[91]

(452) As regards the determination of place for the members of the whole, it decides the geometrical form which the combatants on both sides should assume in the combat.

(453) We leave out of sight at present the forms of detail which are contained in the regular (normal) formation which we shall consider afterwards.

(454) The geometrical form of the whole may be reduced to two types—namely, to the parallel, and to that in concentric segments of circles. Every other form runs into one of these.

(455) In fact, whatever parts are supposed to be in actual conflict must be supposed in parallel lines. If, therefore, an Army should deploy perpendicularly to the alignment of the other, the latter must either change its front *completely*, and place itself parallel with the other, or it must at least do so with a portion of its line. But in the latter case, the other Army must then wheel round that portion of its line against which no part of the enemy's line has wheeled, if it is to be brought into use; and thus arises an order of battle in concentric pieces of circles or polygonal parts.

(456) The rectilinear order is plainly to be considered as indifferent, for the relations of the two parties are precisely alike.

(457) But we cannot say that the rectilinear form only arises from the direct and parallel attack (as appears at first sight); it may also take place by the defensive placing himself parallel to an oblique attack. In this case the other circumstances will not certainly always be alike, for often the new position will not be good, often it will not be quite carried out, &c. We now anticipate this, only in order to guard against a confusion of ideas. The

[91] Clausewitz's definition of strategy, from *On War*, is "the theory of the use of combats for the object of the war," whereas tactics is "the theory of the use of military forces in combat." Where the combat takes place, he says here, is a result of strategy. See Clausewitz, *On War*, vol. 1, book 2, chap. 1, 84–94.

indifference which we see in this case lies only in the form of the order of battle.

(458) The nature of the form in concentric segments of circles (or portions of polygons, which is the same), has been already sufficiently developed; it is the *enveloping* and *enveloped* order.

(459) The question of the placing of the parts in space would be fully settled by the geometrical form of the normal order of battle if it was necessary that some of our troops should be opposed to those of the enemy in every direction. This, however, is not necessary; it is much more a question in each particular case: *should all parts of the enemy's line be engaged or not?* and in the latter case, *which?*

(460) If we can leave a part of the enemy's force unattacked, we become by that means stronger for the contest with the rest, either by the simultaneous or successive use of our forces. By that means *a part* of the enemy's force may have to contend with the *whole of our Army.*

(461) Thus we shall either be completely superior to the enemy at the points at which we want our forces, or we shall at least have a stronger force than the general relations between the two Armies would give.

(462) But these points may be taken to represent the *whole*, provided that we need not engage the others; there is, therefore, an artificial augmentation of our forces, by a greater concentration of the same in space.

(463) It is evident that this means forms a most important element in any plan of a battle; it is that which is most generally used.

Notes

(464) The point now is therefore to examine this subject closer, in order to determine the parts of an enemy's force which in this sense should be taken to constitute the whole.

(465) We have stated (in No. 4), the motives which determine the retreat of one of the combatants in a battle. It is plain that the circumstances from which these motives arise affect either the whole of the force, or at least such an essential part of it as surpasses all the rest in importance, and therefore carries them along with it in its fate.[92]

(466) That these circumstances affect the whole of the force we can easily conceive if the mass is small, but not if it is large. In such case certainly the motives given under *d, f, g* concern the whole, but the others, especially the *loss*, affect only certain parts, for with large masses it is extremely improbable that all parts have suffered alike.

(467) Now those parts whose condition is the cause of a retreat must naturally be considerable in relation to the whole; we shall for brevity's sake call them the *vanquished*.

(468) These vanquished parts may either be contiguous to each other, or they may be more or less interspersed through the whole.[93]

(469) There is no reason to consider the one case as more decisive than the other. If one Corps of an Army is completely beaten but all the rest intact, that may be in one case worse, in another better than if the losses had been uniformly distributed over the whole Army.

(470) The second case supposes *an equal* employment of the opposing forces; but we are only occupied at present with the effect of an *unequal* application of forces, one that is concentrated more at a single or at certain points; we have, therefore, only to do with the first case.[94]

[92] (4) The enemy is moved to [evacuate the battlefield]:
  (a) If his loss is excessive,
      (i) . . . fears he will be overpowered,
      (ii) . . . the object will cost him too much.
  (b) . . . formation of his Army . . . is too much shaken.
  (c) . . . fear excessive loss if he continues the combat.
  (d) . . . order of battle is attended with too great disadvantages.
  (e) . . . taken by surprise . . . or suddenly attacked.
  (f) . . . perceives that his opponent is too superior.
  (g) . . . opponent has too great a superiority in moral forces.
As found on p. 30.

[93] Clausewitz is not necessarily concerned with critical vulnerabilities or, what he later developed in *On War*, centers of gravity, but with vulnerabilities themselves. See *Warfighting*, 45–47.

[94] This is creating and exploiting opportunity. See *Warfighting*, 48.

(471) If the vanquished parts are close to each other, they may be regarded collectively as a whole, and we mean it to be so understood when we speak of the *divisions* or *points* attacked or beaten.

(472) If we can determine the situation and relation of that part which dominates over and will carry the whole along with it in its fate, then we have by that means also discovered the part of the whole against which the forces intended to fight the real struggle must be directed.

(473) If we leave out of sight all circumstances of ground, we have only position and magnitude (numbers) by which to determine the part to be attacked. We shall first consider the numbers.

(474) Here there are two cases to be distinguished; the first, if we unite our forces against *a part* of the enemy's and *oppose none to the rest of his Army*; the second, if we oppose to the remaining part a *small force merely to occupy it*. Each is plainly a concentration of forces in space.

(475) The first of these questions, viz., how large a part of the enemy's force must we necessarily engage, is evidently the same as *to how small can we make the width of our front?* We have already discussed that subject in No. 433 and following.[95]

(476) In order the better to explain the subject in the second case, we shall begin by supposing the enemy to be as positive and active as ourselves; it follows in such case that if we take steps to beat the smaller portion of his Army with the larger fraction of our own, he will do the same on his side.

(477) Therefore, if we would have the total result in our favour, we must so arrange that the part of the enemy's Army which we mean to defeat shall bear a greater proportion to his whole force than the portion of our force which we risk losing bears to the whole of our Army.

[95] (433) How far the assailant may carry the contraction of the front of his position, depends on—

   The size of the masses,

   The extent of the enemy's front, and

   His state of preparation to assume a counter-offensive.

As found on p. 166.

(478) If, for instance, we would employ in the principal action three-fourths of our force, and use one-fourth for the occupation of that part of the enemy's Army not attacked, then the portion of the enemy's Army which we engage seriously should exceed one-fourth, should be about one-third. In this case, if the result is for us on one side, and against us on the other, still, with three-fourths of our force, we have beaten one-third of the enemy's; whilst he, with two-thirds of his, has only conquered one-fourth of ours—the advantage is, therefore, manifestly in our favour.

(479) If we *are so superior* to the enemy in numbers that three-fourths of our force is sufficient to ensure us a victory over half of his, then the total result would be still more to our advantage.

(480) The stronger we are in numbers relatively the greater may be that portion of the enemy's force which we engage seriously, and the greater will then be the result. The weaker we are, the smaller must be the portion seriously attacked, which is in accordance with the natural law, *that the weak should concentrate his forces the most.*

(481) But, in all this, it is tacitly supposed that the enemy is occupied as long in beating our weak division as we are in completing our victory over the larger portion of his force. Should this not be so, and that there is a considerable difference in time, then he might still be able to use a further part of his troops against our principal force.

(482) But now, as a rule, a victory is gained quicker in proportion as the inequality between the contending forces is greater; hence, we cannot make the force which we risk losing as small as we please; it must bear a reasonable proportion to the enemy's force, which it is to keep occupied. Concentration has, therefore, limits on the weaker side.

(483) The supposition made in No. 476, is, however, very seldom realised. Usually, a part of the defender's force is tied to some

Notes

locality, so that he is not able to use the *lex talionis* as quickly as is necessary; when that is the case, the assailant, in concentrating his forces, may even somewhat exceed the above proportion, and, if he can beat one-third of the enemy's force with two-thirds of his, there is still a probability of success for him in the total result, because the remaining one-third of his force will hardly get into difficulty to an equal degree.[96]

(484) But it would be wrong to go further with this train of reasoning, and draw the conclusion, that if the defensive took no positive action at all against the weaker portion of the assailant's force (a case which very often happens), victory would likewise follow in that case also in favour of the assailant; for, in cases in which the party attacked does not seek to indemnify himself on the weaker portion of the enemy's force, his chief reason for not doing so is because he has still the means of making the victory of our principal force doubtful, by bringing into action against it a portion of that part of his Army which has not been attacked.

(485) The smaller the portion of the enemy's force which we attack, the more possible this becomes, partly on account of spaces and distance being less, partly, and more especially, because the moral power of victory over a smaller mass is so very much less; if the mass of the enemy's force which is conquered is small, he does not so soon lose head and heart to apply his still remaining means to the work of restoration.

(486) It is only if the enemy is in such a position that he is neither able to do the one nor the other—that is, neither to indemnify himself by a positive victory over our weaker portion, nor to bring forward his spare forces to oppose the principal attack, or if irresolution prevents his doing so—that then the assailant can hope to conquer him with even a relatively very small force, by means of concentration.

(487) Theory must not, however, leave it to be inferred that it is the defender only who is subject to the disadvantage of not be-

[96] *Lex talionis* is Latin for "The Law of Retaliation."

ing able to indemnify himself properly for the concentration of forces made by his adversary; it has also to point out that *either of the two parties*, either the assailant or the defender, may be involved in such a situation.

(488) The assemblage of forces more than are proportionate at some one point, in order to be superior in numbers at that point is, in point of fact, always founded on the hope of *surprising* the enemy, so that he shall neither have time to bring up sufficient forces to the spot nor to set on foot measures of retaliation. The hope of the surprise succeeding, founds itself essentially on the resolution being the earliest made, that is on the initiative.

(489) But this advantage of the initiative has also again its disadvantage, of which more will be said hereafter; we merely remark here, that it is no *absolute* advantage, the effects of which must show themselves in all cases.[97]

(490) But if we even leave out of consideration the grounds for the success of an intended surprise which are contained in the initiative, so that no objective motive remains, and that success has nothing on its side but luck, still, even that is not to be rejected in theory, for War is a game from which it is impossible to exclude *venture*. It, therefore, remains allowable, in the absence of all other motives, to concentrate a part of our forces on a venture, in the hope of surprising the enemy with them.

(491) If the surprise succeeds on either side, whether it be the offensive or defensive side which succeeds, there will follow a certain inability on the part of the force surprised to redress itself by a retaliatory stroke.

(492) As yet we have been engaged in the consideration of the proportions of the part or point to be attacked, we now come to its position.

[97] Clausewitz's point here is to remind us that initiative, like tempo, is always relative to the enemy.

(493) If we leave out every local and other particular circumstance, then we can only distinguish *the wings*, *flanks*, *rear* and *centre*, as points which have peculiarities of their own.[98]

(494) The *wings*, because there we may turn the enemy's force.

(495) The *flanks*, because we may expect to fight them upon a spot on which the enemy is not prepared, and to impede his retreat.

(496) The *rear*, just the same as the flanks, only that the expectation of obstructing or completely intercepting his retreat is here more predominant.

(497) But in this action against flanks and rear, the supposition is necessarily implied that we can compel the enemy to oppose forces to us there; when we are not certain that our appearance there will have this effect, the measure becomes dangerous: for where there is no enemy to attack, we are inactive, and if this is the case with the principal body, we should undoubtedly miss our object.

(498) Such a case as that of an enemy uncovering his flanks and rear certainly occurs very rarely, still it does happen, and most easily, when the enemy indemnifies himself by offensive counterenterprises (Wagram, Hohenlinden, Austerlitz, are examples which may be quoted here).[99]

(499) The attack of the centre (by which we understand nothing else than a part of the front, which is not a wing), has this property, that it may lead to a separation of parts which is commonly termed *breaking the line*.

(500) Breaking the line is plainly the opposite of envelopment. Both measures, in the event of victory, have a very destructive effect on the enemy's forces, but each in a different manner, that is:
   (a) Envelopment contributes to the certainty of the result, by its moral effect in lowering the courage of the enemy's troops.

[98] Try and identify, if feasible, the *rear* of an adversary's cyber force, the *flanks* in space, the *wings* in the electromagnetic spectrum. What other divisions are possible?

[99] The Battle of Wagram occurred 5–6 July 1809 between the French Army under Napoleon Bonaparte and Austria. The Battle of Hohenlinden occurred 3 December 1800 between the revolutionary French armies and a coalition of Austrian and Bavarian troops. The Battle of Austerlitz occurred 2 December 1805 between the French Army under Napoleon and a coalition of Austrian and Russian troops. All three were French victories.

(b) Breaking the centre contributes to ensure success by enabling us to keep our forces more united together. We have already treated of both.

(c) The envelopment may lead directly to the destruction of the enemy's Army, if it is made with very superior numbers, and succeeds. If it leads to victory, the early results are in every case greater by that means than by breaking the enemy's line.[100]

(d) Breaking the enemy's line can only lead indirectly to the destruction of his Army, and its effects are hardly shown so much on the first day, but rather strategically afterwards.

(501) The breaking through the enemy's Army by massing our principal force against one point, supposes an excessive length of front on the part of the enemy; for in this form of attack the difficulty of occupying the remainder of the enemy's force with few troops is greater, because the enemy's forces nearest to the principal attack may easily join in opposing it. Now, in an attack on the centre, there are such forces on both sides; in an attack on a flank, only on one side.

(502) The consequence of this is, that such a central attack may easily end in a very disadvantageous form of combat, through a convergent counter-attack.

(503) The choice, therefore, between these two points of attack must be made according to the existing relations of the moment. Length of front, the nature and direction of the line of retreat, the military qualities of the enemy's troops and characteristics of their General, lastly, the ground must determine the choice. We shall consider these subjects more fully in the sequel.

(504) We have supposed the concentration of forces at one point for the real attack; but it may, no doubt, also take place at several points, at *two* or *three*, without ceasing to be *a concentration* of forces against a *part* of the enemy's force. At the same time, no

[100] See above from (339) and onward for commentary on envelopments, starting at p. 140.

doubt, by every increase in the number of points the strength of the principal is weakened.

(505) As yet we have only taken into view the objective advantages of such a concentration, that is, a more favourable relation of force at the capital point; but there is also a subjective motive for the Commander or General, which is, that he keeps the principal parts of his force more in hand.

(506) Although in a battle, the will of the General and his intelligence conduct the whole, still this will and this intelligence can only reach the lower ranks much diluted, and the further the troops are from the General-in-Chief the more will this be the case; the importance and independence of subordinates then increase, and that at the expense of the supreme will.[101]

(507) But it is both natural, and as long as no anomaly arises also advantageous, that the Commander-in-Chief should retain direct control to the utmost extent which circumstances will allow.[102]

Reciprocal Action[103]

(508) In respect to the application of forces in combat, we have now exhausted everything which can be deduced generally from the nature of those forces.

(509) We have only one subject still to examine, which is the reciprocal action of the plans and acts of the two sides.

(510) As the plan of combat, properly so called, can only determine so much of the action as can be foreseen, it limits itself usually to three things, viz.:—
    (a) The general outline.
    (b) The preparations.
    (c) The details of the commencement.

(511) Nothing but the commencement can in reality be laid down completely by the plan: the progress demands new arrange-

[101] This is why an understanding of the purpose, the *why* of a task, is imperative; context changes and information, as Clausewitz aptly notes, dilutes.

[102] A reminder, "Commander-in-Chief" refers to the overall commander of the unit.

[103] Up until this point, Clausewitz is describing combat by looking only at the plans and actions of one side, ignoring the interaction with the enemy. Here, he transitions to look at combat's inherent interaction.

ments and orders, proceeding from circumstances: these are the *conduct* of the battle.

(512) Naturally, it is desirable that the principles of the plan should be followed in the conduct, for means and end always remain the same; therefore, if it cannot always be done, we can only look upon that as an imperfection which cannot be avoided.

(513) The conduct of a battle is undeniably a very different thing to making a *plan* for one. The latter is done out of the region of danger, and in perfect leisure; the former always takes place under the pressure of the moment. The plan always decides things from a more *elevated* standpoint, with a *wider* sphere of vision: the *conduct* is regulated by, indeed is often forcibly carried away by, that which is the *nearest and most individual*. We shall speak hereafter of the difference in the character of these two functions of the intelligence, but here we leave them out of consideration, and content ourselves with having drawn a line between them as distinct epochs.

(514) If we imagine both parties in this situation, that neither of them knows anything of the dispositions of his opponent, then each of them can only make his own conformably with the general principles of theory. A great part of this lies already in the formation, and in the so-called *elementary tactics* of an Army, which are naturally founded only on what is general.[104]

(515) But it is evident that a disposition which only rests upon that which is general can never have the same efficacy with that which is built upon individual circumstances.

(516) Consequently, it must be a very great advantage to combine our dispositions *after* the enemy, and with reference to those of the enemy, it is the advantage of the second hand at cards.

[104] Elementary tactics, today, would be basic tactics, techniques, and procedures or standard operating procedures, such as reporting requirements.

(517) Seldom, if ever, is a battle arranged without special regard to individual circumstances.[105] The first circumstance, of which there must always be some knowledge, is the *ground*.

(518) In knowledge of the ground the defender has the advantage in general in an especial degree; for he alone knows exactly and *beforehand* the spot on which the battle is to take place; and, therefore, has time to examine the locality fully. Here is the root of the whole theory of positions, in as far as it belongs to tactics.

(519) The assailant, certainly, also examines the ground before the fight commences, but only imperfectly, for the defender is in possession of it, and does not allow him to make a full examination everywhere. Whatever he can, in some measure, ascertain from a distance, serves him to lay down his plan.

(520) If the defender, besides the advantage of the mere knowledge of the ground, makes another use of it—if he makes use of it for local defence—the result is a more or less *definite disposition* of his forces *in detail*; by that means his adversary may find out his plans, and take them into account in making his own.

(521) This is, therefore, the first calculation made on the enemy's actual moves.

(522) In most cases this is to be regarded as the stage at which the plans of both parties end; that which takes place subsequently belongs to the conduct.

(523) In combats in which neither of the two parties can be considered as really the defender, because both advance to the encounter, formation, order of battle, and elementary tactics (as regular disposition somewhat modified by ground) come in in place of a plan properly so called.

(524) This happens very frequently with small bodies, seldom with large masses.

[105] After distinguishing between planning and combat, Clausewitz goes on to point out that military forces tend to have preferences for how they will fight. This is doctrine. However, the application of doctrine is modified by the dispositions of the enemy, if known, and the ground on which the combat will take place.

(525) But if action is divided into attack and defence, then the assailant, as far as respects reciprocal action, has evidently the advantage at the stage mentioned in No. 522. It is true that he has assumed the initiative, but his opponent, by his defensive dispositions, has been obliged to disclose, in great part, what he means to do.

(526) This is the ground on which, in theory, the attack has been hitherto considered as by far the most advantageous form of combat.

(527) But to regard the attack as the most advantageous, or, to use a more distinct expression, as the *strongest* form of combat, leads to an absurdity, as we shall show hereafter. This has been overlooked.

(528) The error in the conclusion arises from overvaluing the advantage mentioned in No. 525. That advantage is important in connection with the reciprocal action, but that is not *everything*. To be able to make use of the ground as an ally, and thereby, to a certain extent, to increase our forces, is in very many cases of greater importance, and might be, in most cases, with proper dispositions.

(529) But wrong use of ground (very extended positions) and a false system of defence (pure passivity) have no doubt given to the advantage which the assailant has of keeping his measures in the background an undue importance, and to these errors alone the attack is indebted for the successes which it obtains in practice, beyond the natural measure of its efficacy.[106]

(530) As the influence of the intelligence is not confined to the plan properly so called, we must pursue our examination of the reciprocal action through the *province of the conduct*.[107]

(531) The *course or duration* of the battle is the province of the conduct of the battle; but this duration is greater in proportion as the successive use of forces is more employed.

[106] Clausewitz mentions again that the defense needs an aspect of the offense to be effective.

[107] This is a fundamental question for all commanders. When should one deviate from the plan? And if so, to what degree? This judgment is honed through exercises, wargames, virtual reality, and tactical decision games.

(532) Therefore, where much depends on the conduct, there must be a great depth in the order of battle.[108]

(533) Now arises the question whether it is better to trust more to the plan or to the conduct.

(534) It were evidently absurd knowingly to leave unexamined any datum which may come to hand, or to leave it out of account in our deliberations, if it has any value as regards the proposed course of action. But that is as much as to say that the plan should prescribe the course of action as far as there are available data, and that the field of the *conduct* is only to commence where the plan no longer suffices. The conduct is therefore only a substitute for a plan, and so far is to be regarded as a *necessary evil*.

(535) But let it be quite understood, we are only speaking of *plans* for which there are *real motives*. Dispositions which have necessarily an individual tendency must not be founded upon arbitrary hypothesis, but upon regular data.

(536) Where, therefore, data are wanting, there the fixed dispositions of the plan should cease, for it is plainly better that *a thing* should remain *undetermined*, that is, be placed under the care of general principles, than that it should be determined in a manner not adapted to circumstances which subsequently arise.

(537) Every plan which enters too much into the detail of the course of the combat is therefore faulty and ruinous, for detail does not depend merely on general grounds, but on other particulars which it is impossible to know beforehand.[109]

(538) When we reflect how the influence of single circumstances (accidental as well as others) increases with time and space, we may see how it is that very wide and complex movements seldom succeed, and that they often lead to disaster.

[108] This is perhaps the beginning of the command and control philosophy *Auftragstaktik*, known today as mission command. It is necessary to leave some decisions to be made by the commander during execution because they can make those decisions based on real-time data (i.e., what is currently happening) rather than depending on supposition during the planning phase.

[109] Broad, flexible plans are superior to detailed, inflexible ones. This philosophy would later be shared by another Prussian, Helmuth von Moltke (the Elder).

(539) Here lies the chief cause of the danger of all very complex and elaborate plans of battles. They are all founded, often without its being known, on a mass of insignificant suppositions, a great part of which prove inexact.

(540) In place of unduly extending the plan, it is better to leave rather more to the *conduct*.[110]

(541) But this supposes (according to 532) a deep order of battle, that is, strong reserves.

(542) We have seen (525) that as respects reciprocal action, the attack reaches furthest in his plan.

(543) On the other hand, the defensive, through (knowledge of) the ground, has many reasons to determine beforehand the course of his combat, that is, to enter far into his plan.

(544) Were we to stop at this point of view, we should say that the plans of the defensive reach much further than those of the offensive; and that, therefore, the latter leaves much more to the conduct.

(545) But this advantage of the defensive only exists in appearance, not in reality. We must be careful not to forget that the dispositions which relate to the ground are only *preparatory measures* founded upon suppositions, not upon any actual measures of the enemy.

(546) It is only because these suppositions are in general very probable, and *only when* they are so, that they, as well as the dispositions based on them, have any real value.

(547) But this condition attaching to the suppositions of the defender, and the measures which he therefore adopts, naturally limits these very much, and compels him to be very circumspect in his plans and dispositions.

[110] The more detailed the plan is beforehand, the less flexible it is during execution. Flexibility during execution should be maximized.

(548) If he has *gone too far* with them, the assailant may slip away, and then there is on the spot a dead power, that is, a *waste of power*.

(549) Such may be the effect of positions which are too extended, and the too frequent use of local defence.

(550) Both these very errors have often shown the injury to the defender from an undue extension of his plan, and the advantage which the offensive may derive from a rational extension of his.

(551) Only very strong positions give the plans of the defensive more scope than the plan of the assailant can have, *but* they must be positions *which are strong in every point of view.*

(552) On the other hand, in proportion as the position available is only indifferently good, or that no suitable one is to be found, or that time is wanting to prepare one, in the same measure will the defender remain behind the assailant in the determination of his plans, and have to trust the more to the conduct.

(553) This result therefore shows again that it is the defender who must more particularly look to the successive use of forces.

(554) We have seen before that only large masses can have the advantage of a narrow front, and we may now perceive additional motives for the defender to guard himself against the danger of *an undue extension of his plan—a ruinous scattering of his forces on account of the nature of the ground*—and further that he should place his security in the aid which lies in the conduct, that is, in strong reserves.

(555) From this the evident deduction is, that the relation of the defence to the attack improves in proportion as the masses increase.

(556) Duration of the combat, that is, *strong reserves*, and *the successive use of them as much as possible*, constitute, therefore, the

Notes

first condition in the *conduct*; and the advantage in these things must bring with it superiority in the conduct apart from the talent of him who applies them; for the highest talent cannot be brought into full play without means, and we may very well imagine that the one who is less skilful, but has the most means at command, gains the upper hand in the course of the combat.

(557) Now, there is still a second objective condition which confers in general an advantage in the conduct, and this is quite on the side of the defensive: it is the acquaintance with the country. What advantage this must give when resolutions are required which must be made without examination, and in the pressure of events, is evident in itself.

(558) It lies in the nature of things that the determinations of the *plan* concern more the divisions of *higher order,* and those of *the conduct* more the *inferior* ones; consequently that each single determination of the latter is of lesser importance; but as these latter are naturally much more numerous, the difference in importance between plan and conduct is by that means partly balanced.

(559) Further, it lies in the nature of the thing that reciprocal action has its own special field in the conduct: and also that it never ceases there because the two parties are in sight of each other; and consequently that it either causes or modifies the greatest part of the dispositions.

(560) Now, if the defender is *specially* led by his interest to save up forces for the conduct (No. 553), if he has a general advantage in their use (No. 557), it follows that he can, by superiority in the conduct, not only make good the disadvantage in which he is placed by the reciprocal action out of the plans, but also attain a superiority in the reciprocal action generally.

(561) Whatever may be the relation in this respect between the opposing parties, in particular cases, up to a certain point there

Notes

will always be an endeavour to be the last to take measures, in order to be able, when doing so, to take those of the enemy into account.

(562) This endeavour is the real ground of the much stronger reserves which are brought into use in large Armies in modern times.

(563) We have no hesitation in saying that in this means there is, next to ground, the best principle of defence for all considerable masses.

Character of Command

(564) We have said that there is a difference between the character of the determinations which form the plan and those which form the conduct of a battle: the cause of this is, that the circumstances under which the intelligence does its work are different.

(565) This difference of circumstances consists in three things in particular, namely, in the want of data, in the want of time, and in danger.[111]

(566) Things which, had we a complete view of the situation, and of all the great interrelations, would be to us of primary importance, may not be so if that complete view is wanting; other things, therefore, and, as a matter of course, circumstances more distinct, then become predominant.

(567) Consequently, if the plan of a combat is more a geometrical drawing, then the conduct (or command) is more a perspective one; the former is more a ground plan, the latter more of a picture. How this defect may be repaired we shall see hereafter.

(568) The want of time, besides limiting our ability to make a general survey of objects, has also an influence on the power of reflection. It is less a judicial, deliberative, critical judgment than

[111] The problem with planning is that the planner lacks data; they have to guess what the enemy will do and what will happen. The problem with execution is that there is no time to plan; decisions must be made immediately and in a dangerous situation, which will affect the person's judgment. Their solution is to plan as much as possible but also expect to have to make decisions on the spot (and allow subordinates to do so).

mere tact; that is, a readiness of *judgment* acquired by practice, which is then effective. This we must also bear in mind.

(569) That the immediate feeling of danger (to ourselves and others) should influence the bare understanding is in human nature.

(570) If, then, the judgment of the understanding is in that way fettered and weakened, where can it fly to for support?—Only to courage.

(571) Here, plainly, courage of a two-fold kind is requisite: courage not to be overpowered by personal danger, and courage to calculate upon the uncertain, and upon that to frame a course of action.[112]

(572) The second is usually called courage of the mind (*courage d'esprit*); for the first there is no name which satisfies the law of antithesis, because the other term just mentioned is not itself correct.

(573) If we ask ourselves what is courage in its original sense, it is *personal sacrifice in danger*; and from this point we must also start, for upon it everything rests at last.[113]

(574) Such a feeling of devotion may proceed from two sources of quite different kinds; first, from indifference to danger, whether it proceeds from the organism of the individual, indifference to life, or habituation to danger; and secondly, from a positive motive—love of glory, love of country, enthusiasm of any kind.

(575) The first only is to be regarded as true courage which is inborn, or has become second nature; and it has this characteristic, that it is completely identified with the being, therefore never fails.

(576) It is different with the courage which springs from positive feelings. These place themselves in opposition to the im-

[112] This distinction between physical courage and moral courage is also found in *On War*. However, there Clausewitz focuses on physical courage over courage of conviction; here, this is reversed. See Clausewitz, *On War*, vol. 1, book 1, chap. 3, 46–71.

[113] Clausewitz later determines that genius requires *coup d'œil* (literally, "stroke of the eye") and *courage d'esprit*. Genius involves the ability to, in a glance, recognize the situation, and then the resolution to act and follow through. See Clausewitz, *On War*, vol. 1, book 1, chap. 3, 46–71.

pressions of danger, and therefore all depends naturally on their relation to the same. There are cases in which they are far more powerful than indifference to the sense of danger; there are others in which it is the most powerful. The one (indifference to danger) leaves the judgment cool, and leads to *stedfastness*; the other (feeling) makes men more enterprising, and leads to *boldness*.

(577) If with such positive impulses the indifference to danger is combined, there is, then, the most complete personal courage.

(578) The courage we have as yet been considering is something quite subjective, it relates merely to personal sacrifice, and may, on that account, be called *personal courage*.

(579) But, now, it is natural that any one who places no great value on the sacrifice of his own person will not rate very high the offering up of others (who, in consequence of his position, are made subject to his will). He looks upon them as property which he can dispose of just like his own person.

(580) In like manner, he who through some positive feeling is drawn into danger, will either infuse this feeling into others or think himself justified in making them subservient to his feelings.

(581) In both ways courage gets an *objective sphere of action*. It both stimulates self-sacrifice and influences the use of the forces made subject to it.

(582) When courage has excluded from the mind all over-vivid impressions of danger, it acts on the faculties of the understanding. These become free, because they are no longer under the pressure of anxiety.

(583) But it will certainly not create powers of understanding, where they have no existence, still less will it beget discernment.

Notes

(584) Therefore, where there is a want of understanding and of discernment, courage may often lead to very wrong measures.

(585) Of quite another origin is that courage which has been termed courage of the mind. It springs from a conviction of the necessity of venturing, or even from a superior judgment to which the risk appears less than it does to others.

(586) This conviction may also spring up in men who have no personal courage; but it only becomes courage, that is to say, it only becomes a power which supports the man and keeps up his equanimity under the pressure of the moment and of danger, when it reacts on the feelings, awakens and elevates their nobler powers; but on this account the expression, *courage of the mind*, is not quite correct, for it never springs from the intelligence itself. But that the mind may give rise to feelings, and that these feelings, by the continued influence of the thinking faculties, may be intensified every one knows by experience.

(587) Whilst, on the one hand, personal courage supports, and, by that means, heightens the powers of the mind, on the other hand, the conviction of the mind awakens and animates the emotional powers; the two approach each other, and may combine, that is, produce one and the same result in command. This, however, seldom happens. The manifestations of courage have generally something of the character of their origin.

(588) When great personal courage is united to high intelligence, then the command must naturally be nearest to perfection.[114]

(589) The courage proceeding from convictions of the reason is naturally connected chiefly with the incurring of risks in reliance on uncertain things and of good fortune, and has less to do with personal danger; for the latter cannot easily become a cause of much intellectual activity.[115]

[114] In his chapter "The Genius for War," Clausewitz describes how "the two combined make up the most perfect kind of courage." Clausewitz, *On War*, vol. 1, book 1, chap. 3, 48.

[115] This courage is different, but it is related to moral courage. This is the ability to act based on one's beliefs independent from their morality. However, moral courage is a kind of *courage d'esprit*—it is courage of the mind to act based on what is moral.

(590) We see, therefore, that in the conduct of the combat, that is, in the tumult of the moment and of danger, the feeling powers support the mind, and the latter must awaken the powers of feeling.

(591) Such a lofty condition of soul is requisite if the judgment, without a full view, without leisure, under the most violent pressure of passing events, is to make resolutions which shall hit the right point. This may be called military talent.

(592) If we consider a combat with its mass of great and small branches, and the actions proceeding from these, it strikes us at once that the courage which proceeds from personal devotion predominates in the inferior region, that is, rules more over the secondary branches, the other, more over the higher.

(593) The further we descend the order of this distribution, so much the simpler becomes the action, therefore the more nearly common sense becomes all that is required, but so much the greater becomes the personal danger, and consequently personal courage is so much the more required.

(594) The higher we ascend in this order, the more important and the more fraught with consequences becomes the action of individuals, because the subjects decided by individuals are more or less those on which the whole is dependent. From this it follows that the power of taking a general and comprehensive view is the more required.

(595) Now certainly the higher position has always a wider horizon—overlooks the whole much better than a lower one; still the most commanding view which can be obtained in a high position in the course of an action is insufficient, and it is therefore, also, chiefly there where so much must be done by tact of judgment, and in reliance on good fortune.

Notes

(596) This becomes always more the characteristic of the command as the combat advances, for as the combat advances, the condition of things deviates so much the further from the first state with which we were acquainted.

(597) The longer the combat has lasted, the more accidents (that is, events not calculated upon) have taken place in it; therefore the more everything has loosened itself from the bonds of regularity, the more everything appears disorderly and confused here and there.

(598) But the further the combat is advanced, the more the decisions begin to multiply themselves, the faster they follow in succession, the less time remains for consideration.

(599) Thus it happens that by degrees even the higher branches —especially at particular points and moments—are drawn into the vortex, where personal courage is worth more than reflection, and constitutes almost everything.

(600) In this way in every combat the combinations exhaust themselves gradually, and at last it is almost courage alone which continues to fight and act.

(601) We see, therefore, that it is courage, and intelligence elevated by it, which have to overcome the difficulties that oppose themselves to the execution of command. How far they can do so or not is not the question, *because* the adversary is in the same situation; our errors and mistakes, therefore, in the majority of cases, will be balanced by his. But that which is an important point is that we should not be *inferior* to the adversary in courage and intelligence, but above all things in the first.

(602) At the same time there is still one quality which is here of great importance: *it is the tact of judgment.* This is not purely an inborn talent; it is chiefly practice which familiarises us with facts and appearances, and makes the discovery of the truth,

Notes

therefore a right judgment, *almost habitual*. Herein consists the chief value of experience in War, as well as the great advantage which it gives an Army.

(603) Lastly, we have still to observe that, if circumstances in the conduct of War always invest what is near with an undue importance over that which is higher or more remote, this imperfect view of things can only be compensated for by the Commander, in the uncertainty as to whether he has done right, seeking to make his action at least *decisive*. This will be done if he strives to realise all the possible results which can be derived from it. In this manner the whole (of the action), which should always if possible be conducted from a high standpoint, where such a point cannot be attained, will at least be carried in some certain direction from a secondary point.

We shall try to make this plainer by an illustration. When in the tempest of a great battle a General of Division is thrown out of his connection with the general plan, and is uncertain whether he should still risk an attack or not, then if he resolves upon making an attack, in doing so the only way to feel satisfied, both as regards his own action and the whole battle, is by striving not merely to make his attack successful, but also to obtain such a success as will repair any reverse which may have in the meantime occurred at other points.

(604) Such a course of action is called in a restricted sense resolute. The view, therefore, which we have here given—namely, that chance can only be governed in this manner—leads to *resolution*, which prevents any half-measures, and is the most brilliant quality in the conduct of a great battle.

Finis

Notes

ACKNOWLEDGMENTS

First, an apology to Jan Honig, from whom I first studied Clausewitz in depth: I am sorry it took me seven years to finally read *all* of the book, including the appendices. Moreover, without that introduction to the Graham translation, I never would have known of, nor been motivated to publish, this collection. Next, I must thank Doug King who gave me as much leash as is possible, I imagine, in the Marine Corps. I am grateful to have his confidence and hope that this, in return, helps to promote further trust in junior leaders. I also owe an incalculable amount of gratitude to B. A. Friedman, my Clausewitzian doppelgänger. After I first read *Guide to Tactics*, I thrust it into his hands to make sure that it was truly as valuable as I thought it was. He agreed. Next, without the *Strategy Bridge*, this work would not exist. For one, this is a direct extension of an earlier article published there in March 2020. But more importantly, they first took a chance on my work in 2016. Finding a receptive audience, after careful, constructive editing, was a dream; without their direct and indirect support, I would not have had the confidence to embark on such an effort. Finally, Devan Kreisberg has read far too much of my work and without her scalpel the introductory chapter would still be a mess. If it is readable, that is because of her wisdom, but if not, any and all problems remain mine.

GUIDE TO CLAUSEWITZ AND SELECTED FURTHER READING

Part of our hope in this annotated republication of Clause-witz's *Guide to Tactics, or the Theory of the Combat* is to better balance tactical realities and strategic and political desires. As we have asserted earlier, Clausewitz's *Guide to Tactics* is a work that best introduces practitioners to concepts and ideas that he employs and expands on in *On War*. What follows is a point of departure to investigate Clausewitz's other works and works about Clausewitz.

On War is an incomplete philosophical treatise on the question: *What is war?* Its eight books run the gamut of concepts from genius in war (book 1, chapter 3) to defense of swamps (book 6, chapter 20). Below, we present a few different maps of Clausewitz's work that you may use to plot your approach to *On War*—a kind of choose-your-own adventure, if you will. These targeted readings help chart specific themes and provide exposure beyond simply reading the first chapter of book 1.

Clausewitz on the Nature of War

The core of Clausewitz's theory is his exploration of what war is as a phenomenon, found within book 1, chapter 1, of *On War*. He pursues the question *what is war* through dialectical reasoning: proposing a thesis, countering it with an antithesis, and eventually reaching a synthesis. First, he imagines absolute war, which is a pure, ideal state of unconstrained war. He then concludes that it is impossible in reality, and then explores what constrains this idealized war to produce the phenomenon of war as seen in the real world. Some constraining components include human factors, time and space, the availability of resources, allies, probability, and most important, war's subordination to politics. Clausewitz concludes that war is politics with the addition of violent means and not something separate from it. Politics suffuses war at every moment, at every level, and in every place.

Moreover, war is composed of three forces locked in a variable relationship: violence, hatred, and animosity; probability and chance; and its "subordinate nature of a political instrument, by which it belongs purely to the reason."[1] This is known as the trinity, and Clausewitz thought that different participants in war are more concerned with (but not exclusively so) a specific aspect of it: the population with the violence, hatred, and animosity; the military with probabilities and chance; and the government with reason.

Clausewitz on the Character of War (Warfare)

The nature of war, described above, never changes. But warfare —the character of war, or how it is expressed in practice— always changes. Clausewitz uses the analogy of a chameleon that changes its appearance but always remains a chameleon. The rest of book 1 (after chapter 1) delves into warfare, including concepts like the relationship between ends and means, offense and defense, generalship, human factors, danger, and the role of information in war.

Clausewitz on Theory

In book 2 of *On War*, Clausewitz turns to theory itself. During his lifetime, the trend in military theory was the development of mathematics-based rules for military operations that, if followed, would lead to victory. Clausewitz believed that the construction of such a system was impossible. Instead, the purpose of theory was to train the minds of commanders to apply judgment on the battlefield, not to follow prescribed rules.

It is here that Clausewitz divides military theory into two aspects: strategy and tactics. He briefly reviews the history of military theory, defines and compares the use of laws, rules, methods, and principles in theory, and demonstrates how theory should be applied to history.

---

[1] Gen Carl von Clausewitz, *On War*, trans. Col J. J. Graham, vol. 1, book 1, chap. 1 (London: Kega Paul, Trench, Trubner, 1918), 26.

Clausewitz on History

Theory acts as an interface between artificial means of learning war, such as the reading of military history and training exercises, and participating in actual war, which imparts experience. But in the absence of active operations, military history comprises an important facet of professional military education.

In book 2, chapter 6, Clausewitz entreats military students to look at military history critically, dissecting the actions and reactions of historical commanders and testing them for suitability and viability through analysis. Clausewitz then devotes the entire next chapter to the use of historical examples, providing a guide for how to do so effectively. In sum, Clausewitz views the mere reading of military history as insufficient, even as a waste of time. In *Principles of War*, he asserts that "the detailed knowledge of a few individual engagements is more useful than the general knowledge of a great many campaigns."[2] Training the military mind, Clausewitz believes, requires specific and concentrated analysis of military history through the application of military theory.

As of the time of this work, three of Clausewitz's campaign studies that cover Napoleon are available in English: *Carl von Clausewitz: Napoleon's 1796 Italian Campaign, On Wellington: A Critique of Waterloo*, and parts of the chapters "Campaign of 1812 in Russia" and "Strategic Critique of the Campaign of 1812 in France," among others found in his collected *Historical and Political Writings*.[3] Also valuable is his shorter *Two Letters on Strategy*,

---

[2] Carl von Clausewitz, *Principles of War*, trans. Hans W. Gatzke (Harrisburg, PA: Military Service Publishing, 1942), 68.

[3] Carl von Clausewitz, *Carl von Clausewitz: Napoleon's 1796 Italian Campaign*, ed. and trans. Nicholas Murray and Christopher Pringle (Lawrence: University Press of Kansas, 2018); Carl von Clausewitz, *On Wellington: A Critique of Waterloo*, ed. and trans. Peter Hofschröer (Norman: University of Oklahoma Press, 2010); Carl von Clausewitz, *On Waterloo: Clausewitz, Wellington, and the Campaign of 1815*, ed. and trans. Christopher Bassford, Daniel Moran, and Gregory W. Pedlow (CreateSpace, 2015); and Carl von Clausewitz, *Carl von Clausewitz: Historical and Political Writing*, ed. and trans. Peter Paret and Daniel Moran (Princeton, NJ: Princeton University Press, 1992).

which is a critique of two wargame solutions of an imagined invasion of Prussia by Austria circa 1827.[4]

Clausewitz on Training

Clausewitz first saw combat action when he was 12 years old, and his immediate impression was how vastly different training was from the experience of combat. Later in his career, he commented on training exercises, describing them as "mock attacks that had been discussed, carefully planned and rehearsed long in advance . . . with a seriousness that absorbed life completely, with an enthusiasm that bordered on weakness."[5] These heavily prescribed, preplanned training events did not resemble combat at all, lacking disorder, complexity, and unpredictability. Such training could not prepare an army for war and, indeed, Clausewitz was right. The Prussian Army that trained in this manner met Napoleon Bonaparte's *Grand Armée* at the Battle of Jena-Auerstädt on 14 October 1806, where it was crushed.

In *On War*, book 1, chapter 8, written much later, Clausewitz further describes such peacetime exercises as a "weak substitute" for experience. He recommends introducing chance and friction into training exercises to train the judgment of military leaders, rather than their ability to follow a script. Military leaders will have to deal with such stresses in combat:

> It is of immense importance that the soldier, high or low, whatever rank he has, should not have to encounter in War those things which, when seen for the first time, set him in astonishment and perplexity; if he has only met with them one single time before, even by that he is half acquainted with them.[6]

---

[4] Carl von Clausewitz, *Carl von Clausewitz: Two Letters on Strategy*, ed. and trans. Peter Paret and Daniel Moran (Fort Leavenworth, KS: Combat Studies Institute, U.S. Army Command and General Staff College, 1984).

[5] Quoted in Anders Engberg-Pedersen, *Empire of Chance: The Napoleonic Wars and the Disorder of Things* (Cambridge, MA: Harvard University Press, 2015), 116.

[6] Clausewitz, *On War*, trans. Graham, book 1, chap. 8, 82.

Clausewitz on Small Wars

The idea of small wars was nascent during Clausewitz's lifetime. Indeed, the term *guerrilla warfare* came out of the Spanish revolt against Napoleon's rule, which Clausewitz would have observed through news sources. The term alternately meant *partisan warfare*—fighting done by civilian irregulars—and the actions of light infantry troops equipped with rifles and employed as screening, harassing, and reconnaissance forces. Few contemporary theorists examined it in depth. Unsurprisingly, Clausewitz was one of the ones who did, and his ideas on small wars anticipated much later theorists who claimed novelty in the field.

The most accessible work on small wars appears in *On War*, book 6, chapter 26, "Arming the Nation." Although Clausewitz was an instructor in the subject as a young captain and wrote earlier on this subject, this chapter can be viewed as the synthesis of his thoughts. Clausewitz believed that irregular or partisan troops were most effective when employed alongside or in parallel with regular troops, especially as part of a strategic defense against an invasion. Although by the time *On War* was composed, this idea had been put into practice against Napoleon in both Spain and Russia, for proponents of hybrid warfare, this chapter can be taken as its theoretical origin.

Clausewitz on Strategy

As mentioned above, Clausewitz divided warfare into two interrelated parts: tactics and strategy. Where tactics is the use of military forces to win engagements (no matter the size, from skirmish to invasion), strategy is the use of those engagements for the purpose of the war.[7] Here, Clausewitz sets up two conflicting logics: tactics is merely about winning, and usually about the destruction of the opposing forces. Strategy, however, is about the eventual peace. The logic of tactics and the logic of strategy may coincide and agree with each other, but not always. If they do conflict, strategy must take priority. Tactics that do not serve to advance strategy (and therefore peace) is just mindless

---

[7] Clausewitz, *On War*, trans. Graham, vol. 1, book 2, chap. 1, 86.

slaughter, a moral wrong, and a waste of resources. Strategy, therefore, is always occurring and should always direct tactical decisions. "Strategy," Clausewitz writes, "can therefore never take its hand from the work for a moment."[8]

The whole of *On War* is suffused with strategy, but book 3 is specifically about strategy. It was not finalized, and most translations include notes that Clausewitz, had he lived longer, intended to include in the final revision. One clear, overarching theme, however, is that strategy cannot just account for physical forces in warfare, but must also account for moral forces. This is a clear break with other contemporary theorists, who attempted to reduce war to predictive, mechanistic rules grounded in mathematics; appreciating moral forces is one of Clausewitz's great innovations. The book covers concepts like boldness, perseverance, and surprise alongside more traditional ideas like numerical superiority. Importantly, when it comes to strategy, it is not an individual battle that matters. Clausewitz compares strategy to a chain, with individual links composed of movements, positioning, and battles (tactics).[9] Critically, strategy focuses on the effect of a battle's outcome, it's "signification," rather than battle itself.[10]

This chain of strategy must lead somewhere. For Clausewitz, the aim of strategy is the center of gravity. Clausewitz's version of the center of gravity is not equivalent to the one found in U.S. military doctrine (which would be more properly termed a *main effort*). Clausewitz's center of gravity is a strategic concept, not a tactical one, and is defined as "a centre of power and movement, [that] will form itself, on which everything depends; and against this centre of gravity of the enemy, the concentrated blow of all the forces must be directed."[11] The center of gravity is frequently assumed to be the enemy's armed forces, but for Clausewitz that is not necessarily true. In some cases, the enemy army is the center of gravity. In other cases, it is a capital or prov-

---

[8] Clausewitz, *On War*, trans. Graham, vol. 1, book 3, chap. 1, 166.

[9] Clausewitz, *On War*, trans. Graham, vol. 1, book 3, chap. 3, 174.

[10] Clausewitz, *On War*, trans. Graham, vol. 1, book 1, chap. 2, 32.

[11] Clausewitz, *On War*, trans. Graham, vol. 3, book 8, chap. 4, 106.

ince, a commander or king, or any other thing that is politically important. Divining this is one of the many critical judgments placed on a commander in chief.

Clausewitz on Napoleon Bonaparte

Clausewitz had a complicated relationship, from afar, with the man who dominated Europe during his time, Napoleon Bonaparte. Clausewitz's written works tend to compliment Napoleon and his skills as a general. However, he was no fan, even going as far as resigning his commission in the Prussian Army when Prussia was allied with Napoleon to join the Russian Army, which was fighting him. When writing campaign histories that covered Napoleon's actions, he was critical of the version of events presented in Napoleon's memoirs, but defended his decisions at times. For instance, even when writing about the Waterloo campaign in which Clausewitz had personally fought on the opposing side, he attempted to maintain a balanced critical military view, even if he added some poetic ad hominem after Napoleon's defeat at Waterloo: "Here, Bonaparte does not appear to be a great man, but almost as an embittered mediocrity, like someone who had broken an instrument and furiously threw the fragments to the ground."[12] Still, at a time when contemporaries tended to either vilify Napoleon or, like Clausewitz's rival theorist Henri de Jomini, glorify him, Clausewitz tended to view Napoleon with a critical, even-handed clarity. Napoleon embodied the changing character of warfare that Clausewitz's theory of war had to accommodate.

Some Scholars on Clausewitz's Life, Work, and Times

- Peter Paret's *Clausewitz and the State* (1976) traces Clausewitz's career in terms of its relation to political developments in Europe and Prussia, from the French Revolution to Clausewitz's death in 1831. Paret pays special attention to Clausewitz's own thoughts on politics.

---

[12] Clausewitz, *On Wellington*, 160–61.

- Hew Strachan's *On War: A Biography* (2007) looks specifically at *On War*, its composition, publication, and the history of its influence, while also providing a prescient overview of the ideas contained therein.
- Jon Sumida's *Decoding Clausewitz: A New Approach to* On War (2008) looks at *On War* through the lens of other military theorists and their reactions, responses, and critiques of it, including his own.
- Antulio J. Echevarria II's *Clausewitz and Contemporary Warfare* (2007) examines Clausewitzian concepts in light of Clausewitz's methodology to shine light on their applicability to modern warfare.
- Michael Howard's *Clausewitz: A Very Short Introduction* (2002), an essay-length introduction to Clausewitzian concepts, features his trademark clarity and brevity to produce perhaps the best introduction to *On War* in print.
- Clausewitz's works on small wars are compiled, translated, and analyzed in *Clausewitz on Small War* by Christopher Daase and James W. Davis (2015). It includes works on partisan and guerrilla warfare, as well as Clausewitz's lecture notes on light infantry operations from his time as an instructor in tactics.
- Sibylle Scheipers's *On Small War* (2018) contends that Clausewitz's work on small wars is fundamental to understanding *On War*. Tied to the defense as the stronger form of warfare, Scheipers argues that a potential people's war provided the latent means necessary to reestablish the balance of power in Europe after Napoleon's defeat in 1815.
- Anders Engberg-Pedersen's *Empire of Chance* (2015) is a unique reading of the intellectual environment at the turn of the eighteenth century. War, he reasons, is a problem of knowledge. Through a reading of literature, maps, wargames, and other media he explores how military theorists, like Clausewitz, sought to make real what was unknown or unknowable about war.
- The definitive biography of Marie von Clausewitz is Vanya Eftimova Bellinger's *Marie von Clausewitz: The Woman Behind the Making of* On War (2015). Accomplished in her own right, Ma-

rie had great influence on Clausewitz, his career, and his theories, and was responsible for the first publication of *On War* in 1832.

- Charles Edward White's *The Enlightened Soldier: Scharnhorst and the* Militärische Gesellschaft *in Berlin, 1801–1805* (1989) details the military intellectual environment (*Militärische Gesellschaft*) in Prussia prior to its humiliating defeat in 1806. This describes the intellectual foundation, attributed mainly to Clausewitz's mentor, Scharnhorst, for the development of the Prussian General Staff.

- Andreas Herberg-Rothe's *Clausewitz's Puzzle: The Political Theory of War* (2007) is the most comprehensive analysis of the philosophical grounding of Clausewitz's theory of war. Herberg-Rothe proceeds by analyzing book 1, chapter 1, to unravel how Clausewitz's theory moved from seeing war as a duel to war as a "wondrous trinity."[13]

Olivia A. Garard and B. A. Friedman

---

[13] Carl von Clausewitz, *On War*, ed. and trans. Michael Howard and Peter Paret (Princeton, NJ: Princeton University Press, 1984), 89. The Graham translation on which this work is based, however, uses "wonderful trinity."

Selected Further Reading

Aron, Raymond. *Penser la guerre, Clausewitz,* tome 1, *L'âge européen.* Paris: Gallimard, 1976.

———. *Penser la guerre, Clausewitz*, tome 2, *L'âge planétaire.* Paris: Gallimard, 1976.

Bassford, Christopher. *Clausewitz in English: The Reception of Clausewitz in Britain and America, 1815–1945.* New York: Oxford University Press, 1994.

Behrens, C. B. A. "Which Side Was Clausewitz On?" *New York Review of Books.* 14 October 1976.

Bellinger, Vanya Eftimova. *Marie von Clausewitz: The Woman Behind the Making of* On War. New York: Oxford University Press, 2016.

Clausewitz, Carl von. *Carl von Clausewitz: Napoleon's 1796 Italian Campaign.* Edited and translated by Nicholas Murray and Christopher Pringle. Lawrence: University Press of Kansas, 2018.

———. "Carl von Clausewitz: Two Letters on Strategy." Edited and translated by Peter Paret and Daniel Moran. Fort Leavenworth, KS: Combat Studies Institute, U.S. Army Command and General Staff College, 1984.

———. *Clausewitz on Small War.* Edited and translated by Christopher Daase and James W. Davis. Oxford, UK: Oxford University Press, 2015.

———. *Historical and Political Writings.* Edited and translated by Peter Paret and Daniel Moran. Princeton, NJ: Princeton University Press, 1992.

———. *On War.* Translated by Colonel J. J. Graham. London: Kega Paul, Trench, Trubner, 1918.

———. *On War.* Edited and translated by Michael Howard and Peter Paret. Princeton, NJ: Princeton University Press, 1984.

———. *On War.* Edited by Ralph Peters. Translated by O. J. Matthijs Jolles. New York: Modern Library, 2000.

———. *On Wellington: A Critique of Waterloo.* Edited and translated by Peter Hofschröer. Norman: University of Oklahoma Press, 2010.

————. *Principles of War*. Translated by Hans W. Gatzke. Harrisburg, PA: Military Service Publishing, 1942.

————. *Théorie du Combat*. Translated by Thomas Lindemann. Paris: Economica, 1998.

————. *Vom Kriege*, Hinterlassenes Werk des Generals Carl von Clausewitz. Edited by Werner Hahlweg. 18th ed. Bonn: Dümmler, 1973.

Coker, Christopher. *Rebooting Clausewitz:* On War *in the 21st Century*. New York: Oxford University Press, 2017.

Cole, Brian. "Clausewitz's Wondrous Yet Paradoxical Trinity: The Nature of War as a Complex Adaptive System." *Joint Force Quarterly* 96, no. 1 (1st Quarter 2020): 42–49.

Colson, Bruno. *Clausewitz*. Paris: Perrin, 2016.

Cormier, Youri. *War as Paradox: Clausewitz and Hegel on Fighting Doctrines and Ethics*. Montreal: McGill-Queen's University Press, 2016.

Diniz, Eugenio, and Domício Proença Júnior. "A Criterion for Settling Inconsistencies in Clausewitz's *On War*." *Journal of Strategic Studies* 37, no. 6–7 (2014): 879–902. https://doi.org/10.1080/01402390.2011.621725.

Donker, Paul. "The Evolution of Clausewitz's *Vom Kriege*: A Reconstruction on the Basis of the Earlier Versions of His Masterpiece." Translated by Paul Donker and Christopher Bassford. ClausewitzStudies.org. 2019.

Echevarria, Antulio J., II. *Clausewitz and Contemporary War*. Oxford, UK: Oxford University Press, 2007.

Engberg-Pedersen, Anders. *Empire of Chance: The Napoleonic Wars and the Disorder of Things*. Cambridge, MA: Harvard University Press, 2015.

Engberg-Pedersen, Anders, and Martin Kornberger. "Reading Clausewitz, Reimagining the Practice of Strategy." *Strategic Organization* 1, no. 13 (June 2019): 1–13. https://doi.org/10.1177/1476127019854963.

Ford, Matthew. "The Epistemology of Lethality: Bullets, Knowledge Trajectories, Kinetic Effects." *European Journal of International Security* 5, no. 1 (February 2020): 77–93. https://doi.org/10.1017/eis.2019.12.

Friedman, B. A. "Creeping Death: Clausewitz and Comprehensive Counterinsurgency." *Military Review* (January–February 2014): 82–89.

———. *On Tactics: A Theory of Victory in Battle.* Annapolis, MD: Naval Institute Press, 2007.

Gallie, W. B. "Clausewitz Today." *European Journal of Sociology* 19, no. 1 (1978): 143–67. https://doi.org/10.1017/S0003975600005130.

———. *Philosophers of Peace and War: Kant, Clausewitz, Marx, Engels and Tolstoy.* Cambridge, UK: Cambridge University Press, 1978.

Garard, Olivia. "Clausewitzian Deep Cuts: #Reviewing Guide to Tactics, or the Theory of the Combat." *Strategy Bridge*, 23 March 2020.

———. "Lethality: An Inquiry." *Strategy Bridge*, 1 November 2018.

———. "Tactical and Strategic Interdependence." *Strategy Bridge*, 18 December 2016.

———. "Targeting Clausewitzian Judgments: Fusing Precision and Accuracy to Strategy and Tactics." *Strategy Bridge*, 20 September 2016.

Garard, Olivia, and B. A. Friedman. "Clausewitzian Alchemy and the Modern Character of War." *Orbis* 63, no. 3 (Summer 2019): 362–75. https://doi.org/10.1016/j.orbis.2019.05.007.

Gat, Azar. *The Origins of Military Thought: From the Enlightenment to Clausewitz.* New York: Oxford University Press, 1989.

Handle, Michael I. *Masters of War: Classical Strategic Thought.* 3d ed. London: Routledge, 2001.

Herberg-Rothe, Andreas. *Clausewitz's Puzzle: The Political Theory of War.* New York: Oxford University Press, 2007.

Heuser, Beatrice. *Reading Clausewitz.* London: Random House, 2002.

———. *Strategy Before Clausewitz: Linking Warfare and Statecraft, 1400–1830.* London: Routledge, 2018.

Honig, Jan Willem. "A Brief Encounter with Major-General Carl von Clausewitz (1780–1831)." In *The Return of the Theorists: Dialogues with Great Thinkers in International Relations.*

Edited by Richard N. Lebow, Peer Schouten, and Hidemi Suganami. New York: Palgrave MacMillian, 2016, 126–33.

———. "Interpreting Clausewitz." *Security Studies* 3, no. 3 (Spring 1994): 571–80.

Howard, Michael. *Clausewitz: A Very Short Introduction*. New York: Oxford University Press, 2002.

King, James E. "On Clausewitz: Master Theorist of War." *Naval War College Review* 30, no. 4 (Autumn 1977): 3–36.

"On War." *Metropolitan Magazine,* May 1835 and June 1835, 209–13, 252–57.

Palmgren, Anders. *Visions of Strategy: Following Clausewitz's Train of Thought*. PhD diss., National Defense University, 2014.

Paret, Peter. *Clausewitz in His Time: Essays in the Cultural and Intellectual History of Thinking about War*. New York: Berghahn Books, 2015.

———. *Clausewitz and the State: The Man, His Theories, and His Times*. Princeton, NJ: Princeton University Press, 2007.

Pommerin, Reiner, ed. *Clausewitz Goes Global: Carl von Clausewitz in the 21st Century*. Berlin: Carola Hartmann Miles-Verlag, 2011.

Rothfels, Hans. "Clausewitz." In *Makers of Modern Strategy: Military Thought from Machiavelli to Hitler*. Edited by Edward Mead Earle. Princeton, NJ: Princeton University Press, 1943, 93–113.

Scheipers, Sibylle. *On Small War: Carl von Clausewitz and People's War*. Oxford, UK: Oxford University Press, 2018.

Schuurman, Paul. "War as a System: A Three-Stage Model for the Development of Clausewitz's Thinking on Military Conflict and Its Constraints." *Journal of Strategic Studies* 37, no. 6–7 (2014): 926–48. https://doi-org.lomc.idm.oclc.org/10.1080/01402390.2014.933316.

Simpson, Emile. *War from the Ground Up: Twenty-First-Century Combat as Politics*. London: Hurst, 2012.

Smith, Hugh. "The Womb of War: Clausewitz and International Politics." *Review of International Studies* 16, no. 1 (January 1990): 39–58. https://doi.org/10.1017/S026021050011263X.

Strachan, Hew. *Clausewitz's* On War: *A Biography*. New York: Grove Press, 2007.

Strachan, Hew, and Andreas Herberg-Rothe, ed. *Clausewitz in the Twenty-First Century*. Oxford, UK: Oxford University Press, 2007.

Sumida, Jon T. "The Clausewitz Problem." *Army History*, no. 73 (Fall 2009): 17–21.

———. *Decoding Clausewitz: A New Approach to* On War. Lawrence: University Press of Kansas, 2008.

Tashjean, John E. "The Transatlantic Clausewitz 1952–1982." *Naval War College Review* 35, no. 6 (November–December 1982): 69–86.

Tashjean, John E., K. T. Strongman, Geoffrey Till, M. L. Dockrill, David B. Capitanchik, and C. R. Mitchell. "Book Reviews." *Journal of Strategic Studies* 4, no. 2 (1981): 209–19. https://doi.org/10.1080/01402398108437078.

White, Charles Edward. *The Enlightened Soldier: Scharnhorst and the* Militärische Gesellschaft *in Berlin, 1801–1805*. Westport, CT: Praeger Publishers, 1989.

INDEX

ABOUT THE EDITOR

Olivia A. Garard served as an active duty officer in the U.S. Marine Corps from 2014 to 2020. She holds a bachelor of arts in philosophy from Princeton University in Princeton, New Jersey, and a master of arts in war studies from King's College London, United Kingdom. Clausewitz tends to bind her motley thoughts together. She tweets at @teaandtactics.